PRAISE FOR
MY MYSTICAL PATH

"Through her personal story filled with universal truths, Donna Shin-Ward offers healing gifts of grace, comfort, and courage to help readers where they are on their journey. She shows us how to embrace our challenges and transform them into our next level of growth and transcendence in life. I'm deeply grateful for Donna's role in my own life—both personally as a fellow writer and professionally through this book—and I know how much this work can help those who are searching for answers right now. Allow her words to wash over you and help you move forward again."

—CAROLYN CRIST, journalist and co-author of
The New Science of Narcissism

"A tender introspective about a journey of loss and love, filled with engaging insights that describe the human experience. Donna Shin-Ward's story resonates on the deepest level as her memoir speaks to us about encountering modern-day mystics and the power of paying attention to our dreams. *My Mystical Path* artfully weaves Donna's own experiences with her clinical expertise in counseling psychology. This book, like its author, is genuine, vulnerable, and affirming."

—HEIDI SCHREIBER-PAN, PHD, author of *Taming the Anxious Mind: A Guidebook to Relieve Stress & Anxiety*

"*My Mystical Path* demonstrates that those who have experienced trauma, loss, or significant stress can deepen in ways that would not have been possible had the negative encounters not happened in the first place. With clarity, wisdom, and kindness, Donna Shin-Ward shares how psychologically shattering moments in our lives can lead to true spiritual adventures if we are willing to be honest, let go, and become open to new, encouraging teachings about ourselves. Don't be surprised if when you put down this book, after having savored each of its chapters, you have a smile on your face and ask yourself: Why would I ever want to deny my darkness, remain numb, and simply go through the motions each day when God is calling me to honor my goodness and live my life, as well as compassionately express it to others in its fullness?"

—**DR. ROBERT J. WICKS**, author of *The Simple Care of a Hopeful Heart: Mentoring Yourself in Difficult Times*; professor emeritus, Loyola University Maryland

"Donna Shin-Ward begins her story with a shocking diagnosis of cancer at the tender, young age of seventeen. This begins her path to understanding how trauma and the coping strategies of her family impacted her childhood and her early adult relationships. As Donna describes her new, developing self-understanding, she takes you on a journey of struggle yet still finding delight in Spirit. As she continues to grow and take risks, we see the mystical, whimsical, graceful side of her journey. It is clear that she is sharing her own self-awareness of the lessons that came to her in life so that if you desire, you can metaphorically walk in her footsteps to discover your own inner knowing. Donna encourages trust in your inner truth and Divine self. She demonstrates the gift of taking risks is movement toward your own transformation and deep connection to Spirit. Anything can be overcome by taking it one step at a time. What a beautiful, heartfelt read that can expand personal growth."

—**CHERIE LINDBERG, LPC, NCC, ABD**, Brainspotting trainer and consultant

MY MYSTICAL PATH

A Memoir *of* Finding Grace *and* Dignity *in* Life's Hardest Lessons

DONNA SHIN-WARD

RIVER GROVE
BOOKS

This book is a memoir reflecting the author's present recollections of experiences over time. Its story and its words are the author's alone. Some details and characteristics may be changed, some events may be compressed, and some dialogue may be recreated.

Published by River Grove Books
Austin, TX
www.rivergrovebooks.com

Copyright © 2023 Donna Shin-Ward

All rights reserved.

Thank you for purchasing an authorized edition of this book and for complying with copyright law. No part of this book may be reproduced, stored in a retrieval system, or transmitted by any means, electronic, mechanical, photocopying, recording, or otherwise, without written permission from the copyright holder.

Distributed by River Grove Books

Design and composition by Greenleaf Book Group and Mimi Bark
Cover design by Greenleaf Book Group and Mimi Bark
Cover image used under license from ©Shutterstock.com/Olga Korneeva

Publisher's Cataloging-in-Publication data is available.

Print ISBN: 978-1-63299-697-8

eBook ISBN: 978-1-63299-698-5

First Edition

For Christen, Amy, and Sarah
With all my love, thank you for choosing me.

CONTENTS

PREFACE ix

INTRODUCTION: My Hero's Journey 1

PART 1: Companionship 7

    CHAPTER 1: The Lesson of Surrender 9

    CHAPTER 2: Meeting the Divine Mentor 25

    CHAPTER 3: The Call of Consciousness 41

PART 2: Seduction 57

    CHAPTER 4: Be a Truth Teller 63

    CHAPTER 5: Aftershocks and Showing Up 77

    CHAPTER 6: Understanding Trauma 93

    CHAPTER 7: Doing the Work 109

PART 3: Grace 125

    CHAPTER 8: Understanding Grief 129

    CHAPTER 9: Mystical Grace 145

    CHAPTER 10: Loving Yourself 161

    CHAPTER 11: Creating Your Meaningful Life 177

MY MYSTICAL PATH

EPILOGUE 193
ACKNOWLEDGMENTS 195
APPENDIX 197
NOTES. 201
ABOUT THE AUTHOR 205

PREFACE

Your soul came here to struggle with the bitter things of life and squeeze out of them a syrup of sweet inner joy.

RABBI TZVI FREEMAN

We all have a story, and underneath our own story lies a universal story. My hope is that you will find my story inspirational, and it will help you connect with the universal oneness that we all share. I have evolved over the years, embodying life as a daughter, friend, sister, Christian, wife, mother, grandmother, stepmother, student, pastoral psychotherapist, holistic wellness coach, spiritual lover of God, empath, and modern-day mystic.

Now I find myself as an author who wishes to leave a legacy of love to all who find the courage to transform the unexpected in their lives into awakening the perspectives of acceptance, love, and dignity. In these pages, I have written my story of transforming grace to inspire you—your heart and soul—to open up to this amazing gift of grace for yourself.

What do I mean by grace? Grace, to me, is when you feel the sweetest and most subtle assistance of the Divine's Love. It's a gift,

MY MYSTICAL PATH

sometimes called unmerited favor, that is given when you surrender your life, heart, or any difficult situation into the care of the Divine.

It feels like strength and comfort when you are weary or lonely. It feels like a flash of knowing when you need wisdom. It feels like an angel whispering in your spirit to go this way now. This supernatural wonderous grace, which comes from a never-ending source of power, is indeed amazing. Grace offers the ability to forgive the unforgivable, to transform the deepest grief, and the courage to begin again. Actually, when connected to this Divine source, you receive the energetic power to carry out all you feel called to do and be.

As a licensed clinical therapist, for over twenty years I studied in a unique graduate program that integrated psychology and spirituality, which changed my path radically. Having felt drawn for some time, even before entering grad school, to work specifically in the field of grief and loss, I was able to pursue this early in my career. This brought me much foundational learning in what the soul needs to transform through the inevitable losses life brings.

It is said that we teach what we need to learn. Perhaps this has been true for me. Actually, I'm thankful for the lessons and the surprising gifts of grief. Taking this foundation into my work with many who taught me what they themselves needed to learn and heal from led me to study trauma and how it can impact one's ability to mature emotionally and spiritually.

After some traumas of my own—the pain of my second marriage ending and after a time of my own necessary healing, recovery, and contemplation—I felt led to incorporate my specialties into a new niche. Designed for spiritual women of faith to recover from the devastation of narcissistic emotional abuse, I created a program of recovery called Soul of Healing. You see, in my understanding, deep healing happens in a holistic way, and that includes addressing the mind, body, and spirit.

Preface

The Holy Spirit is deeply invested in every pain and challenge that leads us to our growth into wholeness; without this suffering we cannot transcend to our next level of growth, so we must find a healthy way through to move forward.

This is my calling and blessed purpose. After the personal sanctification I have experienced, I feel that if I don't make the healing gifts I have been given come alive to help others, my experience will have been wasted. My purpose is being a guide to help others break the chains that bind and keep them stuck—whether those chains be grief, debilitating symptoms of abuse, depression, anxiety, or any of the other manifestations of trauma. This work and continued learning is what energizes me.

Yesterday my daughter, Amy, said my three-year-old grandson, when asked what was helping him feel better in adjusting to preschool, emphatically answered, "Myself!" Such wisdom from young August.

No doubt he had many people encouraging him and comforting him through the new school experience, but ultimately he decided he had to do it himself. This has been true for me over the years; and isn't it also true for you? As you navigate your way through trauma and challenges big and small, please know that you're not alone. Your Higher Power, your support system, and your close friends—maybe even a therapist—are all cheering you on and offering you guidance, encouragement, expertise, and supernatural strength (which is just a prayer away). But in the end, it is up to you to surrender to unforeseen forces of Love waiting to help you and do the healing work.

There is grace in every part of your story too. Everything life brings us is rich material for us to elevate and to help us transcend our pain so our soul can grow. After my second marriage ended, I vividly remember shaking my head through my tears and pain and saying, "I have to write a book!"

MY MYSTICAL PATH

I could not believe I was yet again facing the grief and the enormous changes of losing another marriage.

But I made it through that grief, and as a bonus, I did write that book! Here it is. I humbly offer it to you. I hope you enjoy stepping into my journey as you read about the peaks and valleys I have delicately traveled. I truly hope the stories in these pages will deepen your life, just as they have mine.

Donna Shin-Ward, MS, LCPC

Introduction

MY HERO'S JOURNEY

One day when I was working with a therapist, with whom I was doing some specialized art and music therapy training along with some personal work, she commented that I was living the hero's journey. I remember feeling strangely curious at the time. I was somewhat acquainted with the work of mythologist Joseph Campbell and his development of the mythical and transformative enlightenment.[1] Yet as I studied the elements and deeper meaning of this perilous journey, I could find resonance with my own journey.

As you read my story here, you will become acquainted with the problems, tests, fears, and tensions that I, or anyone who is called to this universal path, must resolve in order to return home as a changed, equipped, and victorious soul.

I did not make a conscious decision to set out on any kind of adventure of "heroic" proportion. There were spiritual forces of nature that were involved that I believe wanted to be fulfilled and were guiding and moving me forward. Of course, I had a choice to make at every turn, but the power of this hallowed energy seemed to be leading the way. Those many places of feeling the grace to go on and the Love that held me are nothing short of extraordinarily sacred and mystical.

MY MYSTICAL PATH

My mystical hero's journey is divided into three parts. Each part reflects the blessings and challenges of my journey with each of my three marriages. I have chosen an archetype that embodies each husband, because each has influenced my life in a profound way. Along the way in my quest for wholeness, I have discovered that I was being called to a mystical journey to return home to myself. When I say "mystical," I mean my journey was filled with deep communion and a rich inner life with my Beloved savior and our spiritual relationship that continually affirmed to me deep love, mercy, and compassion, along with a magical knowing and trust.

It is sad in some ways that it took these relationship challenges and losses before I could fully experience my full inner potential, but relationship is the divine cauldron for growth—and for that I am grateful. It is interesting also to note that Joseph Campbell insists that the heroic journey is for a man or woman. However, Maureen Murdock, author of the book *The Heroine's Journey*, discusses how the journey for a woman is to recover her lost feminine aspect. "For this means a voluntary descent to the inner world. . . . It involves a time of isolation—a period of darkness and silence learning the deep art of listening: of being instead of doing."[2]

Your own hero's journey will be very different from mine. There will be different archetypes, allies, enemies, and experiences involved. It will be the key lessons and awakenings you learn in each relationship that ultimately bring you to a vibrant relationship with yourself, the Divine, and future relationships. You will find a list of archetypes at the appendix in the back; check it out if you're curious about your own or your partner's archetype. Within all this deep work the blessing is, you will be able to grasp, feel, and know how deeply you are loved and then grow spiritually into all that you were meant to be, and even attract relationships that embrace and welcome divine grace and real, healthy love for self and others.

COMPANIONSHIP

In part 1 of the book, you will learn about companionship. In these early chapters I refer to my first husband as the/my Companion. I am thankful for my first husband's gift of companionship and loyalty to me, and for the time we shared and the gift of our three daughters. When we met, my soul was searching for a love that would feel like security and stability. My desire for a steady and stable Companion to settle down with at this stage of life was a deep-seated need in me that had undertones of desperation. The ebb and flow of simple, everyday married life, including caring for a home and raising children, seemed like the way for me to compensate for the insecurity that I felt growing up. I somehow thought that doing things differently and being successful would make all wrongs right.

SEDUCTION

In part 2 you will learn about the Don Juan archetype. As a woman coming out of the protection and sheltering life with the Companion, I fell prey to my second husband—the classic Don Juan archetype, a man of seduction. On the good days, and even on the hard, grievous ones, vibrant new life and tingling energy pulsated through me as I moved on from the Companion. This left me completely vulnerable to the power of Don Juan's romantic charm and into another spiritual initiation.

In the pages of part 2, I share my confrontation with truth and explain the value of honoring it. I hope it will encourage you to do the same in your own life. The necessity to show up for life when you are vibrating with grief and shock is an art anyone can learn. These chapters are a call to all who read my story to understand trauma and the gifts that can come from doing your work.

GRACE

In part 3, we will learn about Grace, through the Divine Love of my Beloved Mentor, who sustained me at every turn of illness, desperation, and grief—and blessed me with a dependence on the limitless supply of this freely offered cosmic power. The energy of this Love not only offered survival when necessary, but also gave me wings to soar, transcend, and bask in high places—on ordinary days, doing ordinary things. Grace has given me the gift of seeing life, myself, and others through the eyes of Love and compassion.

After two failed marriages and finding myself single in my late fifties, the idea of another marriage was rather disheartening, to say the least. The ending of my marriage to Don Juan devastated me, and I could not see how I would ever recover from that. I'd learned many lessons. The idea of having a relationship without being married felt better now.

Then Grace stepped in, giving me courage when I met my third husband, who embodies the Knight archetype. He personifies a warrior, and in real life he holds a third-degree black belt in taekwondo. He loves history, science, Old Hollywood black-and-white movies, and is knowledgeable about history and politics. He can tell you the name of every animal and plant. He knows each bird in our yard by its song. He is loyal to a fault. We bonded over our past misfortunes and became true friends.

In this last part of the book, I will share with you the necessity of honoring grief and grace and how they complement each other. I will discuss how I believe a life lived with the gift of grace can offer a mystical spirituality, one that has made me feel worthy of Love. I have learned that new beginnings are possible, but not perfect. And the journey is not complete without scaling the heights and wading through the depths associated with living a layered, soulful life.

WHY YOU SHOULD READ THIS BOOK

It has been meaningful to examine my own humble life in the context of Joseph Campbell's Hero's Journey. I certainly don't think of myself as a hero, but when I include myself within Campbell's description of a hero, I fit. He said, "A hero is an ordinary individual who finds the strength to persevere and endure in spite of overwhelming obstacles. . . . A hero is someone who has given his or her life to something bigger than oneself."[3]

Have you, too, encountered overwhelming obstacles? My hope and prayer for you in reading my story is that you will find genuine inspiration in the pages ahead. Joseph Campbell described the Hero's Journey for all of us, and I am grateful for his ability to make mythological stories universal and practical for the ordinary seeker.

For example, you may identify as someone who:

- Is seeking your own awakening moment
- Has limiting beliefs about your past or future
- Is healing from previous grief or trauma
- Wants to focus on personal development and spiritual growth
- Needs inspiration around resiliency, vulnerability, and growth
- Wants to understand more about holistic health and the mind, body, spirit connection

Perhaps you will be inspired to examine your relationships in archetypal ways, as I have here. In the appendix of this book, I have included a list of the twelve major archetypes, for those of you interested in learning more about them.

MY MYSTICAL PATH

If you consider that you have an "operating style" within a relationship that depicts how you approach love and interact with another at a certain time of your life, this knowledge can help you understand archetypal behavior patterns. Our archetypes are a combination of our experiences, biology, temperament, and emotions, and we all have different archetypes that we resonate most deeply with.

Caroline Myss, one of my favorite authors and teachers, states that "working with your archetypal patterns is the best way I know to become conscious of yourself, the effects of your actions, and the need for choosing wisely every day."[4] Her book *Sacred Contracts* is an excellent resource for using the archetypes to "awaken to your divine potential." You can even receive insights into your relationships by learning how to recognize your own archetypes and those of your loved ones.

May the offerings from my own life and the lives of those teachers whose wisdom I share in these pages bring you to your own mystical moments of emancipation and grace.

With my love and light,
Donna Shin-Ward

Part 1

COMPANIONSHIP

Chapter 1

THE LESSON OF SURRENDER

> Mastery leads to freedom from the fear of death,
> which in turn is the freedom to live.
>
> —JOSEPH CAMPBELL

At age seventeen, after being diagnosed with an advanced stage of cancer, I was faced with a new reality. This intrusion eventually brought me to a solemn understanding: We each have the choice to do the best we can with the circumstances we have been given. Some of what is given will be challenging—and possibly change our lives. My diagnosis was no doubt challenging, and as the years passed after my treatment it became more and more clear how the reverberations of my illness were far-reaching. It is our choice to do the best we can with the circumstances we have been given.

When I was diagnosed, I was a junior in high school. My illness did not let me finish that year of school—cancer (procedures, staging, surgery, and treatment) was the next life class I was expected to pass. The memory of that shocking news is still vivid to this day.

I received the news while I was sitting on a dark brown crushed velvet swivel chair, holding the avocado-green landline kitchen phone whose cord stretched out to the living room. When the doctor spoke, I took it all in.

"Some kinds of cancer are curable, and some are not."

You would think a doctor talking to a teenager would be a little more charitable, but a scientist looking at biopsy slides often tells it like it is. This was my new and shocking reality.

> It is our choice to do the best we can
> with the circumstances we have been given.

In that very moment, I was curiously alone. No one was there to see the shock waves of cortisol rushing through my body or to throw me a lifeline of comfort. As I got off the phone, my head was spinning and I felt sick to my stomach. Standing up and reaching for the encyclopedia on the living room shelf, I found the H volume and looked up Hodgkin's disease. The words I saw on the page, at least the ones that I understood, sounded awful. This was a huge, life-changing deal.

MY NEW PRIORITY SETTLING IN

Before receiving my diagnosis, I remember the fear that surfaced in the middle of the night during my first hospitalization. Prior to that, I had been sick, losing weight and energy, and waking up in the middle of the night sweating like I'd been swimming in my bed. I would often fall asleep with my pile of schoolbooks around me. Then one day the left side of my neck expanded like I had swallowed a grapefruit. Initially, the doctors were stumped as the local county hospital went to work trying to diagnose me.

The Lesson of Surrender

Waking up in the middle of the night alone in that semi-dark single hospital room, fear descended, big time. My memory of that moment is mostly a blur, except for this lucid snapshot in my brain. I remember a very pretty and compassionate nurse, who must have heard me stirring or crying, tiptoe into my room. I recall her angelic presence coming in and quietly sitting at the edge of my bed. She held me while I sobbed buckets of that fear out. Sometimes when scary stuff happens, you can feel it deeply. Other times, when the nervous system is overwhelmed, the feelings freeze, and you can't feel a thing. It was so much to feel and take in at seventeen, and that night the pressure was just too great to contain. I am amazed and grateful at how this angel nurse stepped in as a surrogate parent for me.

At first, they thought I might have cat scratch fever or mononucleosis. There were other guesses, too, and with each guess the fear and anxiety grew for me and my family. Eventually, they did a biopsy of my neck and sent it off to the prestigious Johns Hopkins Hospital in Baltimore. My home was not too far away, and we would later be thankful because many road trips for testing, surgery, and treatment were in my future.

After the cancer diagnosis, I became a sick girl in a race to survive as one test and procedure after another became my marathon markers. It was so much so fast, and I had no time to process any of it; but no one really considered that. I only remember going through the motions. No one gave me a choice. Fear had settled in for the long haul, leaving me utterly deflated. I was just showing up for whatever they told us needed to be done.

The race began with many procedures to stage the cancer. How far had that monster gone? One particularly painful test I will never forget was the bone marrow biopsy. They took me into a little room the size of a broom closet. I had no heads-up about what was coming. I was told to lean over, and a needle went deep into my hip bone to extract a marrow sample. If I had had a gun, I would have shot that nurse or myself. It hurt like hell. How many more assaults could my body take?

The major abdominal surgery, an abdominal laparotomy, was a standard part of the staging to see if any organs or lymph nodes were involved. After an infected incision and days of morphine and projectile vomiting, my parents and doctors were unsure if I would pull through. As this was going on, my parents were told it was up to me. They could not control the outcome, nor could the doctors. It was in my hands. And God's. This is when I realized I had been blessed with a strong will that would pull me through any challenge life threw at me.

TREATMENT AND AFTERSHOCKS

After the first tenuous days of my recovery from that surgery, treatment could begin. This included chemotherapy and radiation, with many road trips for Mom and me to Hopkins and sick days at home in bed. Before any of that had begun, I met someone. A good-looking, sweet guy who had mysteriously given me hope during my rough recovery after surgery. We had met at a neighborhood party right after my diagnosis and he wanted to date me.

I remember Mom didn't want me to go out that evening, but I could walk to this party and see some friends. So I said I wouldn't be long. I had never seen this guy before. He and his friend gave me a short ride home. We had been talking and he asked to see me again. I did my best to shoo him away. How could I possibly begin to tell him what my very near future of treatment would hold, when I didn't even know what was in store for me? I think I just told him I was sick or had to have surgery. I can't quite recall.

The Lesson of Surrender

To my surprise, he was still around when I came home from the hospital, and we began seeing each other. It was something fun and wonderful to look forward to—my first love. He was such a sweetheart, coming around to my house and bringing me flowers, which my mom received while I was puking in a bucket. I'd be sick for a day after chemo, and then out with him the next. After all, I was just trying to be a normal teenager.

The readjustment back into mainstream teenage life was complicated and difficult after the physical and emotional shock I'd endured. After my treatment was complete, it felt as if my oncologist gave me a tentative "go free" card. He basically stated that we would see how I did. Was I supposed to be happy, sad, or what? He was not to be my doctor anymore and asked me to send him a birth announcement if I was able to have a child one day.

At seventeen it was not an immanent thought to become a mother, but I had always desired a family. I simply filed that in some part of my brain to deal with later. It was unknown whether I could conceive after taking the harsh toxic medicines my body ingested. I had become attached to this kind doctor and felt a sense of trepidation walking out of the hospital that day, passing all the suffering souls sitting together hooked up to IV poles and receiving chemotherapy. I had done my time there.

I do believe that our health care field as a whole understands more today about how serious illness and surgeries, difficult treatments, and the associated psychological challenges may constitute trauma for patients, which points to the need for the patient to be holistically supported. The saving of a physical life is the priority, but this can often leave the rest of the body and soul hanging by a thread. The reverberations are left to be dealt with later—maybe. The aftershock demands on coping mechanisms can manifest in so many ways.

For me, it basically took the form of denial and rebellion, as I would do anything to prove I was "normal"—like going water skiing when I had a twelve-inch row of stitches in my abdomen. There was no listening to my mom's protests. She tried, but sometimes parents compensate when their kids have been through hell, or they just look the other way.

As I think back on it, that summer feels like a blur. To me, it felt like my family was likely in shock and tiptoeing around me, waiting to see how my treatment would work. I don't remember anyone talking to me about what was happening to me or asking how I was doing. I would come and go as I pleased with my now boyfriend doing all the things that undisciplined seventeen-year-olds experiment with.

> The saving of a physical life is the priority, but this can often leave the rest of the body and soul hanging by a thread.

There was a lot of unspoken tension and disconnection in our home. I know my sister felt like all of their limited attention was focused on me, but it came in the negative tones of yelling and trying to rein in my strong will. I would hear my mother complaining about me and how I was acting. I think my sister must have felt very neglected and afraid. There were no healthy coping skills exhibited to us and no comfort or help given on how to deal with the fear.

If our parents had been more attuned, they would have been able to feel and see the pain my sister and I were in—each in our own way. We were not offered guidance and instead were left to figure it out on our own. This was a common pattern in our home.

After a summer of fun with my boyfriend, I began my senior year of high school. He had been the best drug a girl could ask for to dull the pain, and treatment was finally over. After missing the last several months of my junior year, when I returned for my senior year, I felt like an imposter. My body was there, but the rest of me was not.

Feeling the stares of the many curious eyes as I walked through the halls of that large public high school was more than uncomfortable. Have you ever felt like a spectacle and an oddity? That was me. Their stares spoke what their words dared not to say: *There's the girl with cancer.* Becoming the homecoming queen that year felt like a vote of pity. I had to hit bottom emotionally before I began to climb up and out of that harrowing time.

NO FAMILY IS PERFECT

Your self-esteem and self-acceptance are formed by how deeply you feel loved or unloved. When we are children, this influences how we seek love and whether we feel like an outsider or have a sense of belonging to a tribe and to life itself. That dreadful day the diagnosis came, as I sat at home alone in that ugly chair, I did not feel love—I felt terrified. The second phone call that came in that day was from my mother asking me if I was alright; it felt like a sick joke. She was at work, and for whatever reason, I guess she felt it necessary to be there rather than home with me, especially since she knew I'd be getting a call from the doctor. She called me right after the doctor and asked if I was okay. Her workplace was two miles from our house. To this day I don't understand why she hadn't been with me, and I don't remember asking her.

However, I no longer judge her for that. The ordeal was surreal for her, too. She was my true companion through my illness. My father, on the other hand, was generally absent, distant, emotionally unavailable, and narcissistic. I would come to understand the narcissism and its impact much later.

At seventeen I was trying to find my way and figure out who I was, as most seventeen-year-olds do. This is normal, and having parents at the helm for guidance contributed to a safe passage through the many dead-end paths and dangerous byways a teen can take. While I didn't get this from my parents, I later realized this path was meant for me. Before that realization I often felt that something got screwed up for me, but eventually over the years as I grew I came to accept my unique journey.

My parents did not have a handbook for strong-willed children. When I became a parent many years later, I found advice that resonated with me in a book written by Dr. James Dobson called *The Strong-Willed Child*. Discipline the child but don't break their spirit was the message of Dobson's book, and that became my mantra for child-rearing.[2] Mom lamented that she did not have the same prescription for raising me. She often praised me for my mothering style with my spunky firstborn.

It was obvious she still carried some guilt about her past. My parents were not equipped, educated, or consistently present enough to allow secure attachments to form in my young spirit. However, my grandmother, who lived on our same street, was a great source of unconditional love and security.

My illness was a game-changer for each person in my family, and how my parents coped with it set the stage for how my younger sister and I would cope. We were born to very young parents—young in years and emotional maturity and awareness. Years later, while in treatment with a psychiatrist to help my own emotional self catch up with all the cancer carnage, the therapist offered a bold question that really opened my eyes. She indirectly confronted my parents, who were sitting attentively with me, when she asked me how it felt to have teenagers for parents. *Whoa.* Someone saw and understood. In that moment I felt a nauseating wave of relief and sadness.

The crisis of my cancer affected each of us in our own ways, and my parents did not know how to support me—or themselves, for that matter—in healthy ways. I felt what needed to be talked about had sunk slowly underground. It's just the way it was—my mom and dad were doing what they were capable of. I have empathy for the pain they went through, and I don't blame myself. Or them. I was not in control of this illness or how they responded to it.

The stress of my illness drove the cracks in their marriage into a great divide with a chasm too deep for my parents to sustain. As my treatment was nearing the end, the home that I grew up in was put on the market. Mom and my sister moved into an apartment. And Dad moved into his. When this happened, I was college bound. Sadly, my sweet little sister took the brunt of that move. She was vulnerable and got left alone a lot. When she was fourteen, she found companionship and belonging with a rough crowd of adolescents who were making bad choices. This sent her life on a radically different trajectory than it might have otherwise gone.

Mom jumped into the dating pool and Dad disgusted us with his choice of sleazy girlfriends. I really didn't want anything to do with it all and was finding freedom in my college life—except I had to come back to a home that did not feel like a home. Some part of me was very sad about my broken and unavailable family. It made me determined to one day create a home of my own that would stay intact.

HITTING ROCK BOTTOM

It was the darkness of depression, grief, or a combination of both and the agonizing feeling that life had no meaning that took me down. Loneliness and fear cried for help that day, when I was nearing the end of my senior year of high school, and someone in my family, I don't remember who it was, found me deeply sleeping after taking a bottle of Tylenol. Even the boyfriend couldn't save me—all that I'd been through had just overwhelmed my mind and body and confused my spirit. It was this rag doll's proverbial cry for help.

After getting my stomach pumped, I was sent to the hospital psych ward for a rest. *Ugh—somebody pull the covers over my head and have everyone leave me alone.* I remember my dear grandmother standing by my side wringing her hands; I knew she was in so much pain for me and felt helpless. Emotionally I was full of guilt, shame, and fear. Does it even make sense that, after going through all that nasty survival protocol to live, I didn't even value my life? I felt utterly lost.

Group therapy, a psychiatrist, and a few rounds of doctors later, I was sent back to Hopkins, but this time to check out the hospital psych ward. Imagine a haunted house with scary vacant-looking people walking around talking to themselves and smoking cigarette butts that weren't lit. I knew I was bad off, but this was terrifyingly traumatic. Mom brought in a poster of a lion and a lamb resting peacefully together—a biblical reference—to hang in my little cell. I don't know why, but it brought comfort.

Psychiatrists can be just as scary as oncologists, and the man I was assigned to sure was. He looked like he needed to be admitted himself. His office was a huge mess, and he had several trays of rotting hospital food on his desk. One day (I guess he was using a sophisticated technique) he raised his voice, loudly saying, "You have Hodgkin's disease!" I thought he was really odd. He seemed very stressed and overworked, and did not have the presence with me I understand now as being so healing from a professional. Whatever intention he had of cracking through my assumed denial was weak at best. I was hurting so badly, and his messy office and odd way of being was scary and disheartening.

My boyfriend did come to visit me there in that haunted place, and we got to sit in the stairwell and talk. I don't know what he thought had happened to me, but he was kind. I felt like a bird with a broken wing in a cage, and I just wanted to fly into the life of some normal eighteen-year-old and inhabit her body.

I eventually got out of there, but had to return to therapy as an outpatient. This time the psychiatrist was a youngish woman with a warm face that said, "I care." She became someone I looked forward to seeing, and our relationship lasted for several years. We talked about my assimilation back into regular life.

LEAVING HOME

By the grace of God, I graduated from high school. I never wore a cap and gown but received my diploma. My same boyfriend, three years older than me, was my focus and he stuck with me. The next logical step was to go to college. Without any prompting or encouragement from my parents, I decided to apply to the state university that was an hour away from "home."

I was used to doing what I wanted to do by this time without consulting with my parents, and going to college was not a lot different. They were still in the process of separating from each other, and I was in the process of separating from them. They weren't really opposed to the idea of me going away to college. They were mostly indifferent.

I badgered them until they gave in to buy me a car. My dad, reluctantly, bought me an old VW Bug. He cussed and spewed anger at me while teaching me to drive the manual four-speed. Years later, those flashbacks gave me the patience of a saint as I helped my daughter learn to drive a stick shift.

My daughter "cursed" at me too, not happy with the metallic blue VW Jetta with a sunroof that her dad had purchased from his brother. This was the car she was learning on. "Why would you buy a car like this . . . I hate it . . . I'll never learn to drive it!" she said. I calmly kept telling her to keep trying, she would get it, and she would love it when she did. And indeed, she did. My patience paid off.

Even a strong-willed daughter doesn't deserve the "term of endearment" that my father gave me. "Ungrateful brat" just rolled off his tongue. I doubt he ever gave any thought to the hurt and shame he was depositing in me. I was more than thrilled to pack up my red VW and head off to the University of Maryland and fly with the freedom of a cancer-free bluebird of happiness. So very fortunate was I that all my tests were coming back showing no more cancer present. These tests, X-rays, and blood tests would be a regular occurrence for me for five years, until I could be truly free of the memories of cancer.

I know *abuse* is a strong word, one you may be afraid to claim as part of your own inheritance. It was unbelievably painful for me as I became conscious that what had happened in my own life was indeed abuse. For me the emotional devastation caused by consistently being called harsh, unfair names; by not feeling heard; or by feeling invisible deflated my sense of self, almost like quashing any seedlings of self-confidence that may have been growing in me. Years later, when I had the call and courage to do the work, I had to reexperience that despair and grief so I could heal. I later realized that my parents' emotional abuse had created the perfect environment for complex PTSD.

By my sophomore year at Maryland, I was feeling that the worst of my health struggle was in the rearview mirror. Emotionally, there were still times that felt shaky, but the pain that came when my first boyfriend and I broke up was the hardest to recover from. It took a long time—I had become so attached to him and he knew it. But we were young. He let me down carefully by saying that if we were to stay together, we would end up married, and we both needed to experience more of life.

Easy for him to say.

To this day I am thankful for the power of that young love that helped pull me through my illness. I moved to Nantucket Island after

The Lesson of Surrender

that to work and nurse my broken heart with a dear girlfriend. My family was far away, which felt okay as I overcame my grief. Mom and her new boyfriend did come to visit. This man would later become my beloved stepfather.

EMBRACING SURRENDER

Surrender comes when we understand we are not in control. Unlike the soldier who waves the flag and relinquishes the victory, your surrender assures the victory. When you open yourself up to being in the present moment and the present situation, without resisting, is the best way to feel your truth.

Obviously, I hadn't understood this concept of courageous surrender when I was lying in the basement after an overdose of Tylenol. Nor did I realize that I should look for, and could find, a lifeline. At the time I only felt like a limp rag doll who could not find a shred of strength to hang on to. Asking for help and support was the bravest move I ever made.

Surrender comes when we understand we are not in control.

At this point in my life, I was not connected to my Higher Power. Eckhart Tolle in *The Power of Now* offers a practical approach to surrender: "Do not resist the pain. Allow it to be there. Surrender to the grief, despair, fear, loneliness or whatever form the suffering takes. Embrace it. Then see how the miracle of surrender transmutes deep suffering into peace. This is your crucifixion. Let it become your resurrection and ascension."[2]

Do not resist the pain. Allow it to be there. This is what I have come to know deeply in my bones and embrace for myself and for those I have been privileged to guide. It is not our natural instinct—we resist, we grow numb, we avoid. Instead, try sitting down with it, becoming friends with it, and listening to it. My mom was fond of saying, "This too shall pass." She was right. All you must do is surrender. Move the fear out of the way and jump in free fall, knowing you will be caught. Seek support; it is not a journey meant to be taken alone, although there will be plenty of time spent in solitary seeking.

Have I been angry at my parents in my lifetime? Have I thought my life path may have been different if they'd been more emotionally available or had offered me guidance? Have I grieved well and accepted that I would not be who I am today had I not faced the mountains I traversed? Yes, yes, and yes. Thankfully, parents, although extremely important, are not the only ones who contribute to your inner growth and character.

Can you reflect on the dear ones who have shown you love and encouragement, inspiring you to *be you*? Even those who didn't love you well have had significant contributions because they pushed you to overcome something. Like the hero on her journey who had to overcome trials, dig deep, and find aid from unexpected sources, so do we. Without the adversity, unmet need, or crisis, we cannot prevail and grow.

Discovering and healing the wounds and layers of shame that an emotionally abusive parent or spouse can leave in their wake is no less daunting than traversing an unknown land. But this is the calling of the courageous hero's journey, and it has been one of my loftiest quests.

YOUR CALL TO ADVENTURE

We all have a healing quest to embark on if we are brave enough to show up for it. This spiritual journey of transformation is a high calling into the depth of Spirit and self. As we pass back and forth through challenges and victories, we ultimately succeed and attain the freedom to truly live.

The Lesson of Surrender

It may take years to realize what the unexpected blows of life can reveal about your life and perhaps even give you a purpose. Emotional pain drills deep caverns in your innermost being, where clear refreshing springs of peace and joy can spring forth.

The invitation to surrender may come when you are at your wit's end and don't know which way to go or what to do. Your strength and knowing have come up short, but please don't confuse this with weakness. It is a type of sacred surrender that is not of this earth. But if we accept the invitation, we can dance with the angels and live above the pain of this world.

The invitation may come disguised in many forms of loss or ordeal. When the crossroads of life beckon, it is our choice how we respond. That is what we do have control over. Cancer was a life-changer for me. I had no control over it. Did I surrender to it and its challenges? I did not, not in the way I came to surrender later. At seventeen I just did the best I could to follow what was required. There were more life-changing surrenders in store for me.

FOR EXPLORATION

1. What would it take to not have any regrets about your past, about how things you could not control have shaped you?
2. How have you felt love supporting you along the way?
3. What invitation to surrender might you be feeling now?

Chapter 2

MEETING THE DIVINE MENTOR: BEING OPEN TO THE RADIANT LIGHT OF LOVE

> What good is it for someone to gain the whole world, yet forfeit their soul?
>
> —MARK 8:36 NIV[1]

I know firsthand that having cancer shakes you up, but can it wake you up, too? By age seventeen, the bottom had dropped out for me: cancer, my parents' divorce, and trying to figure out where and to whom I belonged. After my taxing treatment, the real work began of trying to grow up and make sense of life. I felt very much on my own. If you have been through a lot of very emotionally taxing ordeals, I offer this to you: Be open to the radiant light of Love breaking through to set you free—it may surprise you.

As I was shifting back to a "normal" life, deep inside I was also slowly waking up to something. I was not sure what it was, but there was a nudging. At about age eighteen, that summer between high school and college, I started to take myself to Catholic Mass. To this day I cannot tell you why. Perhaps I was seeking some meaning to life and felt vacant after my illness. Or perhaps it was Divine Love pulling on my heartstrings.

But I was a selective soul seeker, as I liked only the folk Mass with the hip guitar music. Hiding in a pew and trying to look nonchalant so that no one could see the tears running down my cheeks was a delicate matter. I just knew I felt better after I left, and the scripture that was proclaimed in those services made an impression. The Bible in Hebrews 4:12 states that the word of God is living and active: "For the word of God is alive and active. Sharper than any double-edged sword, it penetrates even to dividing soul and spirit, joints and marrow; it judges the thoughts and attitudes of the heart."

That verse of scripture really made an impact. It was as if something in me was beginning to activate as soon as I heard it.

> Be open to the radiant light of Love breaking through to set you free—it may surprise you.

THE MENTOR'S EARLY CARE

We were not what I would call a church family in the sense of being devoted or talking about what faith means. We said a Catholic blessing at dinner and Mom said bedtime prayers with us when we were little. Having been raised in the Roman Catholic Church, attending Mass was familiar. My mom was from the Southern Bible Belt and had a Protestant rearing with many family members in the clergy. She married my father and converted to Catholicism. Even though my dad only occasionally attended church—usually on Christmas or Easter—Mom remained faithful to her Christian roots.

She attended a church she was not at home in to be sure my sister and I received the Christian foundation that she'd grown up with. After my sister and I got older and received our last sacrament, Confirmation, in middle school, no one at home attended church anymore. But I am forever indebted to my mom for that early indoctrination.

Sometimes the seeds of faith take many growing seasons to break through. Years later as I sat alone in those worn wooden church pews, it felt familiar to be surrounded by the comforting smell of a place I had visited so many times. It was enough to help this budding young woman feel some life-stirring energy and to inspire me to get on with "regular" life.

In hindsight, I am so grateful for those early stirrings that I now recognize as the grace that kick-started my shaky confidence to move forward.

> Sometimes the seeds of faith take many
> growing seasons to break through.

HELLO, FREEDOM

The freedom and independence I experienced living on a college campus and attending classes where no one knew I had cancer was emancipating. I occasionally attended Mass at the Catholic student center like a good Catholic girl. It did not matter that I was sleeping with my boyfriend; it was all good to me. My best friend and I started to plan a trip across the country after the end of our sophomore year. It was the cool thing to do, and we had adventure in our blood. We waited tables and saved money, and my dad obtained my great-aunt and -uncle's old Chevy Malibu, with low mileage, for us to hit the road. He even had it painted yellow, and we dubbed it the "Creed."

We set out with our AAA TripTik maps, camping supplies, and peanut butter to take us from Maryland to California and back, with stops at our chosen destinations, including many national parks. Leaving the East Coast in the fall gave us some invigorating crisp nights in the KOA campgrounds. We were fearless, strong, and adventurous. Visiting friends at Ohio State and seeing the gateway to the West in Missouri kept us on track. Heading west toward Yellowstone National Park was our target. What a glorious journey awaited.

November 2, 1979, was a life-changing day. I will never forget it. We had spent the day taking in all of nature's splendor at Yellowstone. It was picture-postcard perfect, especially the grand finale. A sunset to beat all sunsets was waiting for us at Jenny Lake along the Grand Teton Mountain range. The surreal majesty we stumbled upon took my breath away. We drank it in, and I couldn't help but notice the chill in the air as darkness settled in. Occasionally, we would splurge at a motel or even a resort, but that was not in the plan that night.

Pulling up to a gas station in Jackson Hole, Wyoming, we spotted a primitive-looking wooden structure with a rickety carved wooden sign that said Rocky Mountain Ministry. For two Catholic college travelers, this looked like a safe place to make an inquiry about a cheap place to stay for the night. I bounded off to knock on the door and was greeted by several young college-aged people, who literally looked like they were glowing. I guess my friend and I had a wholesome glow on, too, after our fabulous day, but their glow was penetrating and engaging.

SWEET SURRENDER

"Do you all know of any cheap places my friend and I could stay for the night?" I asked. With their glowing, warm, and friendly faces, they offered their shelter as a sanctuary from the cold. It sounded reasonable to us. Something about them told us they were safe and kind.

They had only one request—that we attend their Bible study. No

Meeting the Divine Mentor: Being Open to the Radiant Light of Love

sweat; we could do that. After all, I had been attending Mass sometimes, and my friend's family were very devout Catholics. There was nothing to lose, only the gain of a warm, good night's sleep.

Gathering around a table set up for a casual meeting, with everyone in jeans and sweatshirts with worn, written-in, highlighted Bibles, someone offered a prayer to begin our Bible study. We were wide-eyed and trying to seem as cool as they were. The prayer was spoken from the heart, and the leader of the Bible study was talking to Jesus. He was asking Him to come and bless their study and open the "Word" to us. This was foreign and odd, as I had never before seen or heard anyone talk to Jesus like a friend.

Suddenly, I began to feel really warm all over, like some Divine source of Love was pouring hot syrup over my body, and it was seeping into each cell and pulsating through me. It was a feeling of peace and extreme calm, but it also was frightening and unknown. I could tell my friend was experiencing some strange and foreign reaction as well.

Being polite and trying hard to tolerate whatever they were talking about, we excused ourselves and headed to the nearest bar. I collapsed into tears. God had struck me, found me, spoken to me, and told me my life had to change. It was that powerful. All I could say and think was, "I don't want to become a nun!" I wanted to have children if I could. Meanwhile, my friend was also processing everything and assured me there would be other options.

It took a while, but we had the courage to go back to the glowing people and tell them what had happened in that Bible study. They rejoiced. Their prayers had been answered. We did not get it. What alternative world had we stepped into? We stayed with them a few extra days. Like students in a new country, all we could do was listen and observe, while trying hard to digest this culture of joy.

They mapped out God's plan of salvation for us in a way we had never heard. The glowers spoke to us about sin and how it would keep us out of heaven and from having a real relationship with God, through His son Jesus. They showed us scripture like Romans 10:9–10 that said, "If you declare with your mouth, 'Jesus is Lord' and believe in your heart that God raised him from the dead, you will be saved." All we had to do was repent of our wrongdoings, ask forgiveness, and we would receive our helper and friend, the Holy Spirit. They said it was a personal decision.

How could it be that we had never heard this simple formula or understood that Jesus could be our friend—and so easily! It was amazing. And it made sense especially because it filled a hole in me that had been aching for so long. We literally got on our knees, repented of our sins, and gave our lives to Christ.

The change and hope I felt afterward were profound. I thought it must be like the miracle one feels when a baby is born. I now got what those Jesus freaks meant by saying they were "born again."

As I relive that experience by sharing this story with you, I feel a wave of comfort wash over me and am reminded of the verse from 2 Corinthians 5:17 that says, "Therefore, if anyone is in Christ, he is a new creation. The old has passed away; behold, the new has come." Feeling refreshed and renewed, we left there with books, shiny new leatherbound Bibles, and tapes to listen to as we continued on our journey.

Sunsets, salads, and a little Bible reading became our daily ritual. We often questioned each other on what a verse of scripture may mean. This became our new life's work—to interpret scripture and integrate all that had happened on that fateful trip. God was no longer an abstract concept, but my new best friend whom I talked to about everything.

Forty years later I have the same relationship with my Beloved. There was no way we could have imagined or prepared for this transformative twist, and I am forever grateful that we "happened upon" this place.

Surrendering my life to Christ that day on my knees was a huge relief. Something in my being knew God's promises to me were true and the missing puzzle piece was locked in place for me to now make sense of life. New meaning and purpose ushered in newfound joy and deep peace, and it was as if a VIP red carpet had rolled out before us for the rest of our journey across the country.

JOY, SIMPLICITY, AND THE POWER OF A PRAYING GRANDMOTHER

A memorable highlight during our travels was a visit with my maternal grandmother in Magee, Mississippi, as we were heading back east. She and her husband received us with big hugs, collard greens, cornbread, and sweet tea. We sat around their wooden table with a soft breeze blowing through the lacy curtains. The Bible and devotional books that took permanent residence on that well-worn table delighted my heart. I still remember the warm feeling of belonging I felt there with them.

We told them our story of meeting the glowing people who loved and shared Jesus with us and that we had accepted Christ. In the most perfect Southern drawl and with so much emotion—they both had tears streaming down their cheeks—Grandmom said, "Honey, we have been praying for you the whole time." I felt there were no truer words.

The power of a praying grandmother is an amazing thing. We became instantly famous as Grandad marched us down to their local Methodist church to tell the youth group all about our salvation adventure. I was starting to understand that if you have received the joy of the Lord, you were supposed to share it.

Feeling the absolute blessed assurance that life had me and that I was safe, unconditionally loved, forgiven, and intimately known felt intoxicating. I wanted everyone to have what I had. Unfortunately, my family at home did not share that joy. In fact, they thought we had been seized by a cult and brainwashed. They were suspicious of my joy and clearly did not understand how I could feel it so powerfully.

Their distrust did not dampen my spirit, however. I pressed on and found believers who *did* identify with the treasures that came with trusting in God. It took years for my parents to see that this was not a temporary condition. My mother eventually began to call me the rock of the family. It may have taken awhile, but she always came around to understand me. As I previously shared, Mom had the ancestral roots of generations of her tribe proclaiming faith, as the apostles in Christ in converting people to Christianity. My Mississippi grandmother, the youngest of twelve, had been raised by a Methodist preacher father and extended family, with her grandfather being a circuit rider, preaching the Word on horseback across the United States as the country was being settled.

Hafez, the Persian poet, also understood the joy of surrendering your life to God in his playful poem called "Tripping Over Joy." He compares the spiritual path to a sublime game of chess with God where the Beloved just made a fantastic move, with the saint continually tripping over joy while saying "I surrender" and bursting with laughter.

It seemed simple then. Possessing childlike faith and trust, like the chess player in Hafez's poem who can easily surrender to all of life's capricious moves, is the faith that our Creator desires from us—full dependence and trust—as written in Matthew 18:3, ". . . unless you become as little children, you will not enter the kingdom of heaven." What's truly miraculous is to be an adult and return to the innocence, playfulness, and security of a child and being filled with wonder and awe. This was my newfound freedom.

It does not feel that simple today, yet every day I meet with my first love and am filled with strength, peace, and the grace to persevere. Surrendering what you cannot control, or don't know the answer to, can be done with simple words and in a prayer. The problem is often leaving it at the altar. Marianne Williamson's quote, "What you leave on the altar is altered," speaks deeply.[2] Her message conveys that with total surrender of our lives and dreams, we become transformed. "It is then that God can unleash the Universal forces and power of the Spirit to change our hearts and direction, but it takes patience and raw faith to leave it alone and in God's hands."

Developing the art of listening and following can take tremendous courage, because we are wounded and have blind spots and don't always know what is best for us. Seedlings take time to grow, and it can be hard to learn. But nothing is a failure if we learn some lessons in the process. Sometimes holding on to the guilt and pain gives life meaning, but it also robs us of so much.

THE SEEKER

I like to call myself a spiritual Christian. It wasn't always this way. As a younger woman, my vision of the movement of God's Spirit was limited, and I believe putting God in a box allowed me to be feel safe. But I was judgmental of others and myself.

Now, especially after having been shown such mercy and grace, I experience the Holy Spirit as the purest and most powerful love unconditionally overflowing with mercy and forgiveness.

Jesus is my savior and my forever first love. The Divine's Word and Spirit truly rescued me out of a pit of meaninglessness and despair and gave me hope. My life experiences and what I've learned in my studies have also introduced me to the richness of other faith perspectives and practices.

I experience and am trained in Reiki, an alternative medicine known as energy healing. I love the Blessed Mother, angels, and dreams, and

MY MYSTICAL PATH

I pray to some saints and smudge my house with sage. I meditate and do yoga. I have studied world religions, had psychic readings, and enjoy learning about the healing properties of the earth's crystals and plants.

No part of this eclectic Spirit-loving soul could be possible without experiencing the love of Christ, who created this spiritual seeker. I believe Jesus knows my heart and dedication as I continue my spiritual journey. I embrace my free will to trust my discernment, and I believe there is much room for authentic spiritual individuals who have varying stories of redemption.

We don't have to be cookie-cutter Christians. Perhaps we are simply asked to embrace and become the same Love that makes us one.

Today, as I write, our country and world have experienced major losses of life due to the ravaging pandemic of COVID-19. Students have been unable to attend schools, and we've worn masks and kept ourselves socially distant from each other. Systemic racism awareness and protests, some violent, have caused us to turn off televisions and news when children are present.

Some adults cannot bear the news these days. The political rhetoric and landscape are divisive and uncertain. Many clients I work with are fearful and unsure of the state of our world. *Is the world spinning out of control? If so, who is in control?*

My current husband, who is a very intelligent, historically aware educator, tells me there have been many times in history when the world has suffered with plagues, viruses, deaths, dictators, and war. He is right. However, having never lived through any of that, it creates real-time concerns for me regarding my own adult children and young grandchildren.

Perhaps the children of today are living in one of the most necessary and influential times. As Caroline Myss writes in *Intimate Conversations with the Divine*, "Only the Divine could orchestrate such chaos." She adds, "We are meant to be in this together because we are meant to undergo a vast, profound shift of consciousness—together."[3]

"God, where are you in all this suffering?" is an age-old theological and philosophical question. Recently one of my therapy clients, through her deep pain and tears, lashed out at God and described an icy silence she felt when she prays. I held the space for her to grieve. I pray for the souls that I work with, and that helps me.

I know it's common for people to feel unconnected from God. When I think of the dark times in my own life, I marvel that I have never felt forgotten. Since the life-changing Holy Spirit awakening during my travels in college, I have always run toward God—and not away—when the unexpected has happened.

Of course, the problem of evil in the world has occupied the best minds of history, and it is not my place to take that on. My experience tells me, however, that when I have faced darkness and pain in my own life the problems are answered by receiving God's grace and sustaining presence. If I don't feel the sweet surge of grace sometimes, I just know it's time to rest in quiet trust and wait for my next inspiration.

A MODERN-DAY MYSTIC

As a therapist, I love experiential therapies that help my clients delve deeper into their unconscious. I also love paying attention to my own dreams and deciphering the messages to understand what my soul is trying to communicate. God is always trying to get our attention and help us grow into more whole and healthier humans. Direct experience from Spirit informs us, and I do believe this is available to all.

Once you've been enraptured—felt without a doubt that you have experienced God's love for you in deep, personal, and sometimes mysterious ways—the hunger for more never ends. My first husband used to tell me I was special when I wanted him to seek more deeply into his own faith. I have learned to respect that we all approach our spirituality in different ways and times—and it is Spirit's work to seek us, too.

In Sedona, Arizona, one day when hiking in the gorgeous majesty of the red rocks, I felt a oneness within that moment; and in a gesture of bliss I raised my arms to breathe in the magic of that spiritual place. I was transformed in both a spiritual and a literal sense. As hard as it may seem to believe, in that moment I was transfigured into an old Native American woman. I think she was indeed the medicine woman I feel such a kinship with sometimes in the things I like and am attracted to.

This woman, perhaps a guide or a form of me from a past life, is old and wrinkled, with dark skin, dripping with beautiful stone jewelry. She wears leather clothing the color of the red rocks and walks barefoot. She exudes wisdom and love. That day I experienced such awe and rapture, and nothing like that has happened again. It was an extraordinary experience that has made me think deeply of the other lives of my soul. I know I am not alone in these types of stories, especially in a place like Sedona, where there are vortexes described as swirling centers of energy that are conducive to deep healing, extraordinary spiritual experiences, and self-exploration.

Today, I identify as being a modern-day mystic. I think the people moving into this mystical light are increasing. The darkness of this world will not prevail, and these really are exciting times to be alive—if you are part of the rising light. For me this means I can surrender my identity and ego temporarily and enter a realm not of this world. I do it every day: in meditation, or when washing the dishes and looking at the birds outside my window, or when sitting on the beach and watching my grandchildren play. Spiritual music transcends my soul often. My paternal grandmother felt that I had a "direct link" to God when I prayed for her soon before her death. I just know that I can't live without the meaning and life that the Holy Spirit fills me with.

Meeting the Divine Mentor: Being Open to the Radiant Light of Love

One day I heard that a woman who was a very accomplished modern-day mystic and teacher was going to be speaking near me. I had devoured Mirabai Starr's book, *Caravan of No Despair: A Memoir of Loss and Transformation*, written about her journey after she lost her daughter. She has translated and written about the original mystic texts. In an interview in *Oprah* magazine, Starr says that to achieve the divine, sacred experience requires "transcending established belief systems, bypassing intellect, and dissolving identification with the ego self."[4]

I went to see her speak, chant, and dance, and my spirit felt a kinship with her. The dictionary defines mystical as "involving or having the nature of an individual's direct subjective communion with God or ultimate reality."

As a mystical seeker and follower of Jesus, I am never quite satisfied to remain status quo in my faith. I find it amazing how Spirit works through each of us. For example, I'm interested in the afterlife and near-death experiences (NDEs) and reflect deeply on the stories told by those who have come back from the brink of death. At the same time, I still hold an air of guarded mystery around those accounts. A popular book, *Proof of Heaven*, written by Dr. Eben Alexander, a neurosurgeon who had such an experience, did not report a hell in the heaven he experienced but rather a love so deep and palpable that it changed his entire life's work and perspective.[5]

He was not a spiritual man before he experienced an NDE, but he became one. With his scientific knowledge of the brain and human body, he now spends his time comprehending the true nature of consciousness. He states his journey to heaven was a direct path into the heart of consciousness. How much more direct can you get than his account of crossing over for seven days? He discusses how direct experience is key to fully realizing how we are all connected through the healing and binding force of unconditional love. I have seen Dr. Alexander speak twice, and it makes sense that God would use a brain surgeon to help people understand the science and the spirit of consciousness after his trip to the other side.

I still can't help but think about how the little children born into poverty and violence have too much against them to get to this love or healing, at least in this lifetime. I found it intriguing when I discovered that the area where my current husband and I went for a honeymoon was noted for being the place where a Southern Presbyterian mystic and clairvoyant, also known as the father of holistic medicine, opened a holistic hospital overlooking the sea in 1928. We were going there to enjoy a lovely inn and the beach. Before leaving, I ordered this healer's classic biography, *There Is a River: The Story of Edgar Cayce*.

There is way too much to say about his humble life and gift, so I will simply speak to how Cayce's story and accounts impacted my understanding of service and the soul. He was no doubt a healer and a vessel, and Divine consciousness worked through him. He did not choose this or want it. In fact, his gift confused him; and all he wanted to do was help people. He read the Bible faithfully, was an awkward child, and loved Jesus fiercely.

Theological scholars and the most highly regarded medical doctors came to investigate the work of Edgar Cayce. His readings, which began with a health-related focus, evolved to include deeper spiritual questions such as the subject of reincarnation, the solar system, the cosmos, quantum physics, and the life of the soul. I felt my own soul begin to stir deeply as I read his works and understood a new way to connect all that my soul has been revealing to me about God's universal love.

My Christian beliefs were not threatened but broadened as I read these materials. Some people in more theologically fundamentalist circles, including churches I have worshipped in, may call me out for entertaining such possibilities as true; and that's okay. As the Bible discusses in Romans 14 about special days and eating certain foods, and about not judging our brothers or causing them to stumble, we are to act out of love. Being able to love those who believe and act differently than we do may be the biggest test of faith.

UNCONDITIONAL LOVE

I believe it was unconditional love that nudged me and pierced my heart in the Catholic Mass when the Holy Spirit stirred within me, and I believe it was the force I felt in Jackson Hole, Wyoming. This warm, syrupy type of love is also what I feel for my three daughters and my grandchildren. Once you know in your bones that you are loved that deeply, it takes away fear. It doesn't matter if your parents loved you or if your husband or wife loves you—well, it does, but this Love goes deeper. It has the power to heal the wounds inflicted by others on your soul and makes you whole.

> With Spirit, there is joy in the journey.

How have you experienced unconditional love? Do you even believe it is possible? You are fortunate if you have had this experience in your upbringing in a family. Not everyone does. Yet, as we grow into maturity, we may feel a restlessness when the money, prestige, or possessions don't fill the void. Or, like me, perhaps you've had a crisis of health or loss that has sucked the meaning out of life. It can happen at any stage of life, and it is never too late to find this love.

The brave, shiny warriors of life have sought help along the way; they have sought out God. If you do this, you cannot fail—though failure is a relative term. If your soul has grown and you have learned, nothing is a failure. I had to learn this firsthand when I followed my soul and had to make extremely difficult choices in my first marriage. With Spirit, there is joy in the journey.

It is our suffering that stirs the heart of the compassionate Divine and opens the windows of heaven to discharge our angels and unleash the synchronicities and rays of spiritual sunshine. This gets our attention. When this happens, we can suddenly know in our bones that we are not alone. Refinement, growth in our character, and a strengthening of our souls is possible for us if we make the choice to work through the tension and not against it.

FOR EXPLORATION

1. Do you have a "failure" that you can't surrender?
2. How have you experienced mystical, unconditional love?
3. Consider the Divine Mentor's leading in your own life. How has it affected you?

Chapter 3

THE CALL OF CONSCIOUSNESS: AWAKENING TO YOUR TRUE SELF

No one ever told me that grief felt so like fear.

—C. S. LEWIS

While I was sitting on the basement steps trying to hide the anguish I was feeling in the sweet home I had lovingly created with my first husband—with so many dreams of a healthy, intact marriage and happy, secure children who would never know the pain of divorce—a Marvin Gaye song came on the radio. "Mercy Mercy Me" is a song about things not being the way they used to be.

This song resonated so deeply with me, I found it startling. I prayed along with the song: *Dear God, what was happening?*

I heard my husband walk through the kitchen upstairs, and upon hearing the song, he sighed out a spooked "Oh no." He knew I was feeling unsettled in a strange and unfamiliar way. That line about things not being the way they used to be was what I believe he was feeling. How could I communicate to him this new anguish I was feeling when I didn't understand it fully myself?

My life was crumbling big time, or was it me who was crumbling? I had meant every word I said when I uttered those wedding vows. I had a lovely home, resplendent window boxes, and even a white picket fence. Three beautiful daughters lived within those walls. This was my dream come true.

I never could have imagined the deep pull of unrelenting tension and heartache I was feeling. My soul was in major conflict. The deep work of a midlife transition was approaching without any warning, shaking me to the core. I had some concerns about the marriage, but quickly repressing them or clinging to my faith for perseverance helped me keep the scary intruders at bay—for a while, at least.

ANSWERING THE CALL

There was no physical affair, but a very tingly emotional attraction, with butterflies and blushing (which I felt was mutual), to a professor's energy and good looks. This encounter initiated a journey into the cave of a dark night of my soul.

It hit me hard as I encountered so many kindred spirits in a course of study I was engaged in. A force, an initiation, a stretching, and a shattering that had no other plan than to have me face the truth and then grieve. A part of me was literally dying as another part was trying to come to life. After I resisted considering what I was going through, my mother wisely observed: "I think you are waking up."

I experienced an irresistible and undeniable pull at this time, not unlike the descent of the Holy Spirit that ushered in the life-changing

The Call of Consciousness: Awakening to Your True Self

spiritual conversion at age nineteen on that fateful cross-country trip. At that time, the Divine knew I was lost and needed emotional healing to fully recover from a devastating cancer diagnosis and whirlwind treatment when I was seventeen. I wondered, *What was the Divine saying to me now?* I processed this question with the deepest care, the help of many wise counselors, and much prayer.

The call to wake up, heal your wounds, and grow in consciousness sometimes comes in horrible ways. I could not avoid this movement, this life-force, this invigorating and daunting momentum within me; it was far bigger than I was. It came when I felt like I had reached the time, with my youngest daughter beginning school, to answer another call—this time into a unique graduate school program integrating psychology and spirituality.

So I said yes to becoming a Clinical Pastoral Psychotherapist. This was a solid way to serve God.

Yet by doing so my marriage would fall apart. The changes I was experiencing required that I be truthful with myself and really get to know and understand my motives and intentions regarding the choice I had made about marriage to him.

> The call to wake up, heal your wounds, and grow in consciousness sometimes comes in horrible ways.

I felt a lack of emotional and spiritual connection with my husband. Some may say I felt unequally yoked in this marriage. I realized, too, that there was also a loss of connection within myself. I was growing in such deep ways, healing old wounds, and I was afraid this journey was going to pull me farther apart from him. We did not have much in common other than our children.

Looking back, the incoming students had fair warning. At the orientation for my graduate program, the chair stated that some of us might not finish the program. He also stated some of us may get divorced or change careers. I knew it was a rigorous program, but I thought I was immune to whatever he was foreshadowing.

EARLY DREAMS AND PRECIOUS DAUGHTERS

Up until that point, all I ever really wanted was to be married and to be a mom. I had begun college majoring in education. But when just a few semesters away from obtaining my degree, I left. My new marriage took us out of state with my husband's job transfer, and I felt ready for something new.

In fact, after getting settled in Amish country in Pennsylvania, I enrolled in the nearby university so I could keep plugging away at that undergrad degree. Then I became pregnant early in the marriage, which was much more exciting to me than anything a textbook could offer.

Unfortunately, I miscarried that pregnancy, and I became acquainted with a new brand of grief. Not being sure I could even have children made the miscarriage doubly devastating. Any woman who has lost a child to miscarriage knows the obsession of becoming pregnant again. It feels like the only thing that can take that pain and heartache away. To this day, I have so much empathy for women who deal with miscarriage and infertility. It is a silent, disenfranchised grief with complexities that are mostly unfamiliar to others unless they feel it firsthand.

During my first marriage I had three miscarriages that no platitude could comfort. And I also had three healthy daughters, who are the absolute joy of my life. I consider them all miracles. However, when my first daughter was born, the presence of the Holy Spirit returned. My daughter was born a few hours before sunrise in a long, relatively normal first labor. I was tickled pink to hear the baby cry, before we even knew the sex of the baby. And then we learned she was a girl! She is exactly what I was hoping for. Our Christen looked like a tiny fresh angel.

Once I got settled in a hospital room to grab some much-needed sleep, my husband went home. I was awake in the room when they brought her to me. The love in that room was palpable. I held that baby for hours, with the grace and love of God flowing through and encircling us. At one point, I remember being a little afraid to open my eyes. I thought I might see the blazing light of Christ standing right before me.

The first few days at home with baby Christen brought similar moments where I felt like I was literally dripping with that warm sweetness I'd felt during that cross-country college trip. After the birth of my second daughter, Amy, I was full of anticipation to experience that same bliss I had after the birth of my first daughter. There was absolute joy, but this time there was no Holy Spirit rapture like I had with Christen. I was a little confused, but it was okay. Our third daughter, Sarah, came almost seven years after Amy. After this birth I experienced great joy, but again, there was no palpable anointing of the Holy Spirit like the first time.

Christen was a strong-willed little girl once she hit eighteen months, and at times was very taxing to raise. Not all girls are sugar and spice; some are aggressive and have temper tantrums galore. Today she is one of the dearest and most thoughtful young women I know and a great mom to her own spunky daughter. Once, when we were going on vacation while she was a toddler and I was at my wit's end with her, I went to speak to a priest at our church.

I cried and poured my heart out to my priest and told him how I felt like a failure as a mom. But I also told him about the joy I'd experienced when she was born. He validated my experience of anointing and said he really was not sure what it meant, but he assured me I was not alone in raising her—the Divine would always be watching over us.

Because of this blessing I received after her birth, there was a part of me that feared maybe something would happen to her. Perhaps the Divine was simply revealing to me the magnitude of this gift, especially after I had been so sick as a teenager and was told I may not be able to have children. It is still a mystery to me. I am just so very thankful each day for her and for her sisters.

THE COMPANIONSHIP OF A HUSBAND

My first husband, and the father of my children, was a good man. He created a lot of stability in my life and allowed me to pursue anything I wanted—have children, plan the vacations, and go to grad school. The thing he and I did best was parent together. I was the stronger disciplinarian for the girls, whereas he was comfortable being more passive and dependent. He was usually fine with my parenting decisions. It's crazy to think that in almost nineteen years of marriage, we never really had a fight. On the other hand, I now see this as conflict-avoidant and unhealthy. The blame is not one-sided, as we both shared some responsibility for this dynamic.

There were plenty of times he could have stood up to me and said no, but he didn't. I came to understand that his general way of being was passive and he was generally not emotionally available. They were very different people, but I recognized my own father had been mostly emotionally unavailable. My husband had difficulty asserting his own needs, just as my mom had. Feelings of familiarity are comforting even in the disconnection. In fact, it is not uncommon to unconsciously be attracted to someone with characteristics like one, or both, of our parents. In doing this, we *may* be able to heal an unmet parental need.

I happily whistled along through these days, taking care of little ones, collecting recipes, and making a lovely home, even when there was little money. It filled a deep need in me for security and fulfilled my naturally nurturing spirit. Those were sweet days, and my girls all feel that they had happy, secure childhoods.

I do believe, however, that I was masking a low-level depression under it all, which was later confirmed by a therapist.

FINDING YOUR TRUE SELF

Donald Winnicott, a psychoanalyst and pediatrician, introduced the concepts of the false and true self. He said, "The true self, also called the real self, is our spontaneous and natural self-expression, a sense of being alive in mind and body that allows us to be genuinely close to others."[1] Winnicott believed that the false and true selves developed in infancy and were based on the interactions with primary caregivers.

The infant reacts to how a caregiver responds to him or her. Ideally, a parent will honor and allow the baby's spontaneous and genuine reactions to the world. If the baby fails to receive consistent, open-hearted parenting to develop and express his or her true self, the false self will become his or her dominant personality.

Many clients I have seen in therapy, and many—I believe—who never make it to therapy, are on a quest to find their true self just as I was. This involves doing your own work, especially with regard to becoming more self-aware about your defense mechanisms. It's hard work that involves grieving the loss of your true self, understanding how she got lost, and welcoming her back. When my first marriage unraveled, I began to understand how my false self was showing up.

I was a dedicated mom and homemaker when my girls were young and growing up. I had a deep faith that inspired my days. I loved being a mom, and I worked very hard to make everything appear wonderful.

MY MYSTICAL PATH

One day, a friend accused me of being a Pollyanna—someone who is unreasonably optimistic and tends to see—and believe—only the good in others. It can come off as ingenuine. Her comment really made me think. Was I really that naive, happy person who presented a false self? Maybe I was just content and peaceful, and she didn't get that. Or maybe I was a soul connected to my Mentor, full of trust and receiving grace.

As I began to do my work and wake up to myself in my late thirties, I realized my over-the-top joy was a mixture of both. It was important for me to appear happy and have the perfect home and family to defend against shame, sadness, and discontent in my marriage. If any unhappiness or depression started to surface unconsciously, I'm sure I worked hard to keep a lid on it.

My sister was confused and sad when my idyllic-looking family and marriage ended. I know that I had been a motivating role model for her as a mother and homemaker when we didn't have a model family of our own to look to. However, she later told me she sometimes hated to call me and hear how wonderful everything was. Listen to what others say about you. The mirror they hold up can be revealing.

Feeling that unhappiness and restlessness would bring up too much pain and uncertainty, I hid it—even to myself. That worked neatly until I went to graduate school, when my true self screamed to come home, and I could not contain the truth anymore. Turns out, I had been unconsciously repressing my anxious discontent by exaggerating how wonderful everything was. The Pollyanna attitude hadn't been genuine.

> Listen to what others say about you.
> The mirror they hold up can be revealing.

I'm much more of a truth teller today, thank God. It took a lot of energy to keep up the facade of the false self. Facing the truth and excavating your true self can rock the proverbial boat, but sometimes it is necessary for your own personal growth.

LEARNING TO SPEAK YOUR TRUTH

Training in a diverse graduate counseling program where I was becoming equipped to help others, it was necessary for me to help myself first. I believed, based on all the contemplation I did at that time, that I could not have reached my true self in my marriage to my husband, who has many of the traits of the Companion archetype; who, although loyal and unselfish, has the characteristic of providing a service, symbolically speaking, to a personality (me) who has a stronger personality or nature.

The Companion will allow, walk alongside, one who is trying to complete their own mission. This I am truly grateful for. However, I longed for someone I could look up to and respect with their own strong identity. I do, however, absolutely believe you can grow, heal, and still find yourself in a marriage. I sadly could not find that path with him. I now understand our differences at many levels and have come to see how my growth and his were on divergent trajectories.

This is not uncommon, nor is it something to grieve over. As stated in 1 Corinthians 13:12, "For now we see only a reflection as in a mirror." I trust God to one day bring these moments from my past into the fullness of understanding.

Speaking the truth first to yourself can be the hardest. My husband and I went to counseling for a short time with a liberal Catholic nun. With much trepidation I had to confess to myself that my heart was not with this man any longer. It took tremendous courage for me to tell him that I was attracted to a professor in graduate school. I was trying to make a point to my husband and help him understand what was happening to me.

I know now that I chose a horrible and cruel way to broach this subject. I never acted on that attraction, but for him it seemed like the ultimate sin. Hurting this faithful Companion took enormous courage on my part—almost superhuman, it seemed. I'd never done anything like it before. Later, it took massive self-forgiveness and the grace of God's mercy and compassion to get me through the crushing grief of this lost dream of a happy marriage and the pain it caused him and my girls.

I got it. I knew he could be rigid in his values and the integrity around them. I respected that, but regrettably, I had lost respect for him. And when respect is lost, a loss of love often follows.

I prayed vigorously that God would change my heart. It took more than three years of absolute grief and anguish before I could discern my truth in our marriage. He said he didn't know me anymore, and I believe he was right. I was changing.

I felt broken and heavy with grief.

There were very few people who understood the transformation that was taking place in me. Interestingly, spiritually inclined people understood. The faculty in my graduate program understood. But my mother and family did not. This caused my mother such anger toward me that it was almost the death of our relationship.

However, thank God for a mother's love, because in the long haul, it made us closer. It took time and created some testy and very hard moments between us, but I was clear as I moved forward that I was not changing my mind. The intuitive process of uncovering my truth was certain. Once you know your truth, nothing can change it. After all the counseling I received, prayers I had uttered, self-compassion I had gained, and belief that God had compassion on me too, I ultimately decided to grieve my losses and begin a new path.

I had unshakable faith that I could get my girls—and myself—through the grief and the changes with Divine grace—and be better for it. This was my goal and vision but there was still great grief. I also felt that my husband would be happier with a woman who he was more compatible with and who would love and adore him. I prayed he would find that.

One day, while sitting in my favorite blue prayer chair communing with my Beloved, the phone rang. It was the nun my husband and I saw briefly for counseling, whom I had not talked to for some time. Our energy, through Spirit, had connected, and she had a message she wanted to share. She told me that if I had to leave my marriage, it would be hard, but grace would be with me.

That was it. I was dumbfounded. When I went in tears to my favorite parish priest, he listened compassionately. Then he, sadly, gave me his blessing to leave my marriage. He didn't see how I could stay with all the eruptions seeking growth coming up within me and plans to be in the healing profession. He had compassion for all of us.

I felt enormously thankful. And fortunate. Surely, I couldn't expect everyone in our lives to have such mercy and grace. I felt like I was on some kind of yellow brick road, following it to my true home.

And honestly, the only place this home could be found was within me.

THE LESSONS OF ANGER

The ancient Greek philosopher Socrates, when asked to reduce all philosophical commandments into one, replied, "Know Yourself."

I've heard it said that not until we are lost do we begin to find and really understand ourselves. I would like to add that only if you take the time to do the work of self-reflection, open yourself to feedback, and practice vulnerability and humility, is it possible to begin to understand yourself.

A failing marriage was the perfect occasion to see myself, twice—with my Companion husband first and more deeply with my second husband. It's easy to blame the other person and become bitter, and sometimes it really is the other's actions that are mostly responsible for a failed relationship. But you also play some part in its dissolution.

I learned this when my second marriage failed.

A spiritual teacher of mine shared something unexpected when that happened. She called it a "master spiritual lesson" to be able to take responsibility. Blaming becomes easier when you are working through a deep painful passage of grief and the anger feels like fiery lava burning into the core of your pride and ego. It flows into the direct path of the other to account for all your pain. I was so hurt and angry at my second husband, but I was also angry at myself for allowing these feelings to linger for so long and for letting my daughters down—again.

However, you must allow yourself to experience and feel the anger.

Feeling the searing energy of anger will allow you to shift to the next stage in your grief process. This anger must become sorrowful enough to help you, the grieving soul, begin to look inward. Some people never reach this place of sorrowful anger.

Anger is an enormously powerful emotion. The emotion of anger can provide tremendous energy to right wrongs and change things for the greater good. But when you allow it to control you, it can lead to negative, destructive actions such as emotional, verbal, or even physical violence. Anger can be unconscious and displaced, too, coming from a past wound or offense in another or in yourself.

The other side of anger is sadness. Anger is the fortress that protects the soul from unfathomable sadness. It is often well defended because it feels like a tsunami ready to let loose and demolish you; but it will not. It's really the fear that is in control here. Anger and sadness are God-given and God-created emotions that can clear away the debris of grief and open new space for new awareness, wisdom, and depth.

It's important to allow the energy of these feelings to move you like a surfer riding a wave. I remember carrying a weight of sadness for so long after my anger at my second husband subsided. It just throbbed in me like a dull toothache.

OWNING YOUR SHADOW

A favorite book of mine is *The Prophet* by Kahlil Gibran. My copy came from my childhood home, and it's old, worn, and has been tenderly loved. Gibran's artistry in the spiritual realm is penetrating: "And a woman spoke, saying, Tell us of Pain. And he said: Your pain is the breaking of the shell that encloses your understanding. Even as the stone of the fruit must break, that its heart may stand in the sun, so must you know pain."[2]

Grief and pain are inescapable, but they are also the vehicle for our healing and consciousness. Life is a paradox. When my dream life crashed with my Companion husband, there were days when I was red-hot angry. *How can it be that I have everything I want, and it is not enough? How could I knowingly hurt my children, my husband, and myself like this and dismantle the family I worked so hard to create?*

At the same time, days full of vigor and new energy buzzing through my veins were present, too. I often asked myself: *What is happening to my life? God, what do you want from me?*

> Grief and pain are inescapable, but they are also the vehicle for our healing and consciousness.

MY MYSTICAL PATH

During that time, I had two dreams that I will never forget. One featured the professor from grad school who I was attracted to, walking toward me with a bright, multicolored dog. The other was a little house with window boxes bursting with vivid, gorgeous blooms. In the deep grief of losing my dream of an intact family, my unconscious was flourishing—bursting with blooms—and this seemed to be a positive sign. Dreams are powerful.

The dream about the professor, to me, symbolized that life was teaching me how to walk with faithfulness and loyalty to myself. It was not literally the professor but my Mentor who was calling me to heal and directing me to wholeness. Earthly people can carry energy that initiates inner spiritual healing. Symbolism and dream work were ways I stayed informed about this new territory of my journey toward the next stage of consciousness, and it was exciting.

In *Owning Your Own Shadow*, Robert A. Johnson spoke to this adventure to consciousness and wholeness. I devoured his books like spiritual candy during this time. He writes:

> The ancient alchemists understood this process. In alchemy one goes through four stages of development: the nigredo, in which one experiences the darkness and depression of life; the albedo, which one sees the brightness of things; the rubedo, where one discovers passion; and finally, the citrino, where one appreciates the goldness of life. After this is the pavanes, the peacock's tail that contains the preceding hues. One cannot stop this process until one has brought it to the pavanes, that concert of colors that contains everything.[3]

There it was! The colors of the rainbow dog the professor was walking with toward me. The synchronicities are real when on this path.

My second husband, who typified the Don Juan archetype, bought notecards with peacocks on them for thank-you notes after our wedding. Remembering the peacock tail Johnson described, I thought it was a sign that I was where I was supposed to be—right in my colorful and promising future. I was so in love and happy with him, I felt I had been given a gift. I was later to learn the gift was not him, but the deeper healing that was waiting for me, which came from more grief, pain, and suffering.

The wave of growth felt relentless. Whatever path I had stepped on took every bit of courage, heart, and brains this Dorothy needed to find her way home from all the tests inside my own Oz.

We do tend to repeat unhealthy patterns from childhood, partnering with people who frustrate us in familiar ways. Success and mutual growth are possible in transforming those frustrations within a relationship into new ways of understanding and relating—if both people can risk vulnerability and own their projections. The biggest offender is the one who is not able to see when they project their own disowned shadow and emotions onto others. Without doing your own work, you remain in the darkness of your own unknowing.

SELF-ACCEPTANCE

We all want and deserve acceptance from those we love, but we first must work with and accept what is coming up in us instead of giving in to procrastination and distraction or leaving a trail of crap behind us for another to clean up and recover from.

Taking responsibility for yourself is a master spiritual lesson. We are wise to take responsibility, but sometimes things just aren't your fault. You are not in control of others. But you are in control of yourself, as well as the choices you make to understand yourself and the impact an unhealthy parent, spouse, or family member may have had on you.

Abusive people hurt. They cause shame and self-doubt and contribute to the development of the false self—especially if the abuse was early in life. They negatively color the way you see yourself.

Many of the dear ones I've listened to in therapy, who have suffered any kind of abuse, come to the raw and very painful truth that, at their core, they feel deep shame. They feel unworthy.

I know firsthand how wretched that feels. Grief is always the way out. With it comes healing and clearing medicine. At some point in therapy, grief will come up. Don't be afraid to explore the darkness that takes up space or comes over you. There is gold in there just waiting to shine. Find an experienced traveler who knows the way and can guide you through your pain. Once you get to the other side of pain and understand its teachings, there will be lasting jewels for you to wear and own.

FOR EXPLORATION

1. What loss has been your greatest teacher?
2. How have you allowed grief to transform you into deeper consciousness, like a jewel that shines from your inner self?
3. How can you take responsibility for yourself in a situation that may be challenging you right now?

Part 2

SEDUCTION

After several years of being on my own, focusing on my new career, creating a cozy home, and being the best mom I could be, I began to feel ready for more. I met and fell in love with my second husband—the classic Don Juan archetype. Like the mythical Don Juan, he had a sensual and smooth air about him. On the good days, and even on the hard ones, vibrant new life and tingling energy pulsated through me as I moved on from the Companion. This new openness left me completely vulnerable to the power of Don Juan's seductive charm.

I longed to share my newfound vitality and ability to love more deeply with someone—in a whole mind, body, and spirit kind of way. Perhaps, he was a test to see how discerning I could now be. I even considered, after recognizing the darker, covert side of him that caused me so much hurt, that maybe this relationship was my karma for leaving my first marriage.

His Don Juan intensity, our chemistry, and his romancing of me and my girls utterly swept me off my feet. His generous, attentive, and fun-loving ways made him quite the romantic enticer, and I allowed myself to be carried away in a fairy tale. I did not have the wisdom to understand this kind of man, nor did I understand what love-bombing meant at that time. Eventually it became necessary to stand up to him to share a hurt or need.

Trying to relate anything other than what, I surmised, made him feel like he was doing a good job in our marriage became a problem. My attempts to bring things up only caused trauma for me as the gaslighting, shaming, and blaming began, which eventually made me physically ill. My discovery journey of wising up left me feeling very alone and without a partner.

My truth, as I came to understand it, was that because my second husband was aware that I'd felt a lack of connection with my first husband, he relied on an approach that brought excitement, attention, and newfound happiness to me. It was just his way of being. I was in love, and he seemed to know exactly what he was doing to my romantic heart and exactly how to channel his sensual energy into every word and gesture. Just as the sex addict is empowered by a need for control, I came to believe that his goal was to gain control of me for his own use.

His sensuality was my weakness, and the Don Juan archetype will take advantage of that, play with it, and enjoy it at his convenience—at least until he gets bored and the conquest has been made. This is exactly what I felt after the intoxicating honeymoon period was over and the dismissals and emotional hurt and fear began to affect my feelings of safety. I went from walking on air to feeling like a deflated life raft trying to stay afloat.

Yet I am thankful for the time I spent with Don Juan, even though I developed a physical illness and suffered an emotional collapse from the stress in the marriage. We had wonderful, magical times together that felt true for me at the time. It's hard to know if he really loved me the way I loved him. I have concluded that he loved me as much as he was capable of loving, until I did not supply him with the admiration and service he seemed to need.

From my spiritual perspective, nothing is ever wasted. The lessons I learned have made me stronger. They've helped me in service to others who find themselves in need of recovery from similar entanglements. I think my girls, too, have been enlightened about the reality and danger of this covert archetype.

Divine love took me deeper into dependence with an amazing grace that got me through the days where I was racked with pain, confusion, and trying to heal from the trauma I suffered. It was a roller-coaster relationship, and long after he was gone, I was left trying to piece myself back together. I never knew I could be courageous enough to say no to this complex, capricious man whom I'd loved, and then work through the trauma and cognitive dissonance that I was left with. But I did work slowly through it when I was faced with the recovery needed.

This strength is seared into my soul now. By the grace and sustaining energy given by my loving Mentor, I passed through this supreme ordeal scared, but also very much alive and well. Mystical love from a higher dimension was holding me.

In chapters 4 through 7, I emphasize the value of truth through my own defining moments and how truth is so healing and valuable to honor. May my story bring you courage to be true to yourself.

Chapter 4

BE A TRUTH TELLER: THE CHALLENGE OF SPEAKING YOUR TRUTH

> God is spirit, and his worshippers must worship in Spirit and in truth.
>
> —JOHN 4:24

The truth is unequivocally big. It is what every therapist is hoping their client can be brave enough to get in touch with for themselves. It is yours alone and it's highly personal. It is the key that can unlock a creaky old door that has been shut tight out of fear, unable to welcome the penetrating and revealing light.

Revealing the truth lets the light begin to fill the cracks, and it sometimes comes with startling and unanticipated revelations and emotions. It is best to honor this healing truth in small doses, so it is not blinding but instead intriguing and informative. Speaking the truth to yourself can be hard. You need heroic courage—and oftentimes the support of others—to unpack, understand, and trust your truth.

LISTENING FOR TRUTH

Your experiences and your encounters with others are unique to you. We want others to hear us and understand what we are saying or feeling—but they may not. This could be because they have not lived what you have, or they don't listen well, or they are not educated in a specific area.

We learn so much from listening to others, but we first must listen to ourselves. It may take time to come to your truth about something important in your life and that's okay. I believe in Divine timing, as many pieces need to be aligned.

Relying on a true confidant or a soul friend, one who knows you so well and shares a spiritual connection, a therapist, and even God, who knows you better than anyone, to bring your questions and anguish to light when wrestling with the inner conflicts is essential. I have been journaling ever since I can remember. My many multicolored, tattered leather journals have been filled with heartfelt words—each tear-stained page filled with prayers, petitions, and praises captured in earnest. These are the private landscapes of my inner life.

> We learn so much from listening to others,
> but we first must listen to ourselves.

After time has passed and hard-won lessons have rearranged my character and understanding, I am ready to dispose of the older records of life's refinement and create a bonfire with holy smoke to allow the new phoenix in me to rise to freedom with the wisdom of new truths.

I often suggest clients write down what's happening in their lives and record their feelings to help bring full expression and clarify their truth. Much can be gained from this practice. Sometimes we just need to hear ourselves say our truth aloud.

How do you really begin to listen to yourself? Your body is always speaking. Emotions are always offering clues to your truth if you are receptive enough to hear it. This can be challenging when the feelings are difficult, as in grief, but their energy longs to be acknowledged and moved through to shift you to the next place of awareness or clarity. Befriend all that your body and soul are trying to communicate to you. While it may not be easy, truth is always on your side.

Being a truth teller and truth seeker is brave.

LISTEN TO YOUR BODY

The words "listen to your body" play on repeat like a record player stuck in the well-worn groove of a favorite song. I regularly utter them to my clients. I can recollect phases of my relationship to Don Juan where my body was speaking loudly to me. I learned to listen eventually when I was told by a doctor that I had an incurable disease. The first vibrations I experienced with him were probably a warning, but to me the excitement was a green light, and I failed to heed the dim warning light.

What woman doesn't like to be love-bombed? After just a few dates, a basket of flowers came to my office that hardly fit through the door. They must have cost a fortune. The ladies in the office gasped. He would drive great distances at all hours of the day or night to leave presents or sneak in a visit. Text messaging was just coming into vogue and my phone at work would ping all day long with his sweet talk.

At one point I quipped, "I'd like to work in your office; it sounds like fun there." He replied quickly, alluding to having better plans for me. I should have listened to the shudders in my body when I read that text. Hearing comments like this now are a huge red flag. But back then it felt exciting and put the oxytocin in my brain on overdrive.

I was thankful for the opportunity to learn later about attachment injuries from childhood and how our magnetic attraction and personalities created the perfect storm, but I had to live through intense downpours and mighty winds to get to my truth by processing the meaning of it all.

I believed in us. I believed in love and in my ability as a superhuman feminine spirit to be able to create a beautiful, loving marriage and stepfamily. Sometimes you just can't see or trust who someone really is, especially if they work overtime in the beginning trying to hide it and study you to become everything they think you want them to be. This was what my experience and my research led me to believe. Please be careful out there . . . there are wolves in sheep's clothing who will tear you apart. You may have sensitivities and wounds that make you vulnerable to covert abuse.

I lived with narcissism and emotional abuse in my childhood. My father was an emotionally unavailable and abusive father. He was overtly narcissistic, which can be just as damaging as being physically abusive. It can take a long time to put all the pieces together if you have a blind spot. To heal, you must become educated on what is showing up so that you can understand what you are experiencing. I did not heed the red flags when I encountered Don Juan—and they were there.

As Kelly McDaniel in *Ready to Heal* writes: "Relationships that start out intense, unpredictable, or frightening, may feel like true love. For women with normal neurochemistry these indicate danger or a probable heartache. But for a trauma survivor, the adrenaline that goes with dramatic people feels normal."[1]

After becoming physically ill from stress, confusion, and heartbreak, I had no choice but to pay attention to my body. It was a frightening state of exhaustion that felt like what I imagined a nervous breakdown to feel like. My nervous system could not take the continual sucker punches I experienced, coming at me in words or deeds that felt like disrespect and tests to see how I would react. My own welcoming flags of healing and self-love were then waving me to take a time-out.

Sometimes I had to travel to get away and find a place to rest, pray, and help my nervous system to relax. I had a lot to process physically, emotionally, and spiritually, and kept my Divine Mentor and grace as my closest companions.

Driving back to visit my former "little blue house," as the girls and I called it, rouses a disturbing memory. A "For Sale" sign greeted me in the front yard. I had purchased this little house after my first marriage ended. After I had moved into Don Juan's home, I could not afford to keep it, so I eventually put it on the market. However, when things got very hard with him, I would drive up to our "little blue house" to find peace.

It had been my sanctuary after my first marriage ended, and was a new home away from home for my girls. My youngest exclaimed, "Buy it!" after seeing it for the first time. The little Cape Cod had window boxes, a front-porch swing, and a screened-in porch with a hammock. My daughter Sarah drew the sweetest, happiest picture of the front of this little house with bright, multicolored flowers spilling out of the front window boxes. She was a precious seven years old then.

Driving back there early into the marriage, my body and heart were so heavy. I could never have imagined what was happening to me. The terrible pain from the bladder disease I was suffering from had become chronic. A urologist told me it was incurable and ordered several surgical procedures to bring some relief. They didn't help.

I felt Don Juan often acted like the hero when I had to go to the hospital, gathering as much of the family as would come to support me. His actions and words seemed to say that he did not want to take the blame or responsibility for any of my stress. My manual on the symbolic and emotional messages of physical diseases stated this about mine: I was pissed off. The pain would flare up after I felt an injustice, or we were disconnected from a fight. It was not hard to tell what my body was saying.

The part of me that felt like a medicine woman, interested in natural health, took front and center by directing me to heal my body with remedies such as: vats of green juice made with bitter greens simmered on the stove; naturopathic medicine; supplements, kinesiology, acupuncture, alkaline water, no acidic food, no coffee, no alcohol . . . I was literally detoxing my body.

Emotional stress causes great dis-ease, which creates acidity that produces a potentially toxic environment in the body to welcome mysterious diseases. I lost a lot of weight in my determination to heal myself. I am grateful to this day that some of the healthy habits and knowledge I acquired in my desperate research continue.

On this particular day I arrived at the little blue house armed with the supplies to give myself a coffee enema, and just try to gain perspective. The sweet house was empty and seemed sad without me and my girls living there. I proceeded to get set up, smudging the kitchen and lighting a candle. The horror of opening the pantry is still much too vivid. The white wire shelves were empty except for the legion of mice moving frantically about. I hate mice, and I can't think of anything worse to make me run for the hills.

After seeing the mice, I grabbed a box and filled it with a few things to take down the road back to the house I was trying hard to make a home with Don Juan. Working so fast, I left an 8x10 wedding photo of Don Juan and me on the roof of my car. After peeling out of the driveway I heard a thud behind me that I pulled over to check out. Our once-cherished wedding photo was cracked with broken glass across the frame. I thought it was probably a sign that this marriage was doomed.

I had done a lot of research for answers into what I was dealing with in that crazy-making marriage before checking myself into a holistic treatment center after the gentle prodding of my very wise daughter. She said, "Mom, stop diagnosing him and take care of yourself."

After the first time I left, moving my youngest and myself into a nearby rental house, I was on the verge of a full-blown nervous breakdown. My life's blood was completely depleted. I was shaky and lost. My body was in trouble.

By this time, I was certain of his very complex personality and felt something was off, but I could not let go of him.

HARD-WON LESSONS

The obvious reason that I couldn't let go was that I still believed in the sanctity of marriage and had fallen hard for a man that I loved, promised vows with, and had created a blended family with. The thought of having one failed marriage was unthinkable, but two—dear God, that could not happen.

I thought he was my "meant to be" for life, and I wanted that more than anything. I had prayed hard asking for guidance before those nuptials, and in that moment things felt blessed and alive with so much promise. He was charming, caring, generous, fun, went to church, and was a great dad. He was good to my girls. He worked very hard. I didn't think he took very good care of himself, but I was going to help him with that.

We worked, each in our own way, to blend our families and create a "Brady bunch." It felt like true love, and we had many wonderful times together until the earthquake tremors of disbelief and confusion started for me. I began to feel dismissed often and felt his attentiveness wane.

We left our little blue house and moved into his house shortly after the wedding. It was my decision because the commute, about fifty minutes, was getting to be too much. I think he would have been happy with us staying there, and in hindsight I probably should have. We could have had a weekend marriage, but this did not fit into my ideal of what marriage was. He promised we'd buy our own house, but the market took a dive, so it didn't happen. My youngest cried to me, asking for our own house. I felt her pain, but we stepped up as best we could.

I transformed that already established house into a warm, cozy home. His former life in his first marriage inhabited those walls, and his kids were born there. He alluded to the house being, before my touches, like a dormitory with milk crates. Before two of my three daughters and I moved in, it had been a fun house where he juggled being a professional—working days, nights, and sometimes weekends—with being an involved, doting dad. My sense was that there was not much discipline or order. His kids really seemed to appreciate my care and creativity and welcomed the homey touches I brought in.

I was adaptable but I needed his support. I was counting on that GPS he promised for my car to learn my way around the new area. My memory recalls that he often said things and then forgot. Tearfully one day I pulled into a gas station to get directions in this new hometown, and shook my head, saying, "Where in the hell am I?" The question had symbolic meaning.

When I asked him about the GPS he'd promised, he looked at me like I was asking for the moon. It made me feel ashamed. The look and feeling were familiar to me. My dearest friend, a good listener, told me, when I was in a seemingly impossible place with him, that our dynamics brought up the same pain I felt in my childhood.

I shook and quaked with fear, anger, and tears, through many dismissals and projections. I sensed a growing rage beneath his surface if I challenged him or had a different opinion. He denied being angry, but I would sometimes hear one of his sons asking him why he was so angry.

According to experts, nonverbal cues make up 70 percent to 93 percent of our communication. I came to believe he wanted me to stay

Be a Truth Teller: The Challenge of Speaking Your Truth

home and be a mostly quiet and content homemaker to him and his children, as he and his kids continued living the life they had before we came, without skipping a beat. He was very devoted to his kids and, in my opinion, was overindulgent trying to make up for lost time when he did not have them. If you have ever tried to blend a family, you know the challenges that can arise.

He did like that I was a Pastoral Counselor, but when I wanted to open my own practice, it felt like he fought me on everything related to it. He seemed to like being in control, and I felt like I had no control. Despite his protests, I opened that practice anyway, and it was successful.

I had left my dream job, specializing in grief and loss in a hospice setting. My youngest daughter finished her last year of middle school commuting to her old school. I allowed so many things to happen that I now deeply regret. Thankfully, she fared well and today is a smart, wise, and capable young lady. I thought she would have great opportunities in our new area. Her resilience and success in a new high school were amazing. She will tell you how much she loved high school and the new area. Yet I know my increasing uneasiness, tension, and flare-ups of physical pain and anger were very hard on her. I have had to forgive myself for all the changes I put her through.

After frequent upsets with this second husband, feeling like I could literally pull my hair out with frustration, I often got in my car and headed to the drive-through at Starbucks. I'd then park in a quiet favorite place near a river. Mom and I had many memorable phone conversations from my car. She'd listen and try so hard to say the right things. She gave me her blessing and said if I had to leave the marriage, everyone would understand. She said it sounded like he had CEO disease—her husband, my stepdad, was a CEO and she was referring to his way of wanting to be the boss in everything.

Yet, I remained damned determined to make it work for several more years, even after her death. I prayed for a sign about what to do. I remember weeping in the hospice, sitting on my husband's lap when we were losing her. I recall him later hinting about how much that made him feel like a man, which confused me, because I thought he already was. It was a difficult time for me, and I felt truly supported by his presence. He was always good in a crisis.

In my opinion, and after many fights and roller-coaster moments with him, I came to feel the differences in our ability to communicate—namely his lack of empathy in our often-circular conversations. The morning we married, I remember taking a good long look at myself in the mirror while waiting for the service to begin. I think behind those eyes was some normal apprehension, but I trusted I could do this. The joy that day, along with the live musicians singing our favorite operatic music, felt amazing. And the smiles on each of our kids' faces as they processed down the aisle holding hands confirmed it was good. The girls carrying roses with ribbons spilling over in their bouquets that matched their turquoise-blue tropical print dresses and those adorable boys with crosses around their necks made us proud. The candles we all lit together as a new family and the blessings we received just could not be untrue.

GETTING PUSHED AWAY

I had to admit that I came into this relationship as a trauma survivor from the emotional abuse I experienced in childhood, and the issues I endured in my first marriage. I had done a lot of "daddy" work before this marriage, trying to work on the remnants of anger and grief I still held about my father. But the issues with my Don Juan were a new kind of trauma.

After I had taken an important time-out for myself, I came back with new strength and knowledge. But I was just not strong enough to walk away. So, I went back to him with hope and prayer, but it just didn't work.

The offenses felt worse—almost as if to punish me and confirm the necessity for me to preserve what was left of myself. I have compassion for both of us in these memories. Our attempt to move and buy a house of our own failed terribly. It seemed to become all about money then—one day he even said so. He agreed to spend on certain things, then chastised me for it later. He accused me of stealing from him. It became scary, and we fought all the time.

Leaving the second time for good, with the shame of two failed marriages and bigger griefs to heal, felt unreal. It seemed like I had too many lessons to learn. A constant question in my heart was: *What are you asking of me, God?*

In my experience and in my version of the truth, when I got to be too much of a challenge for him, made him get too close to his own wounds, or became too demanding or needy, he began to push me away. So while I'd say I was pushed away, he might say I left. I think if a person wants to play the victim, it's easier to blame it on the other person for leaving.

The prevailing understanding among professionals is that a person with narcissism will manipulate a situation to make it impossible for the other person to stay. This is known as "the discard." They play the victim card like an ace. When I was moving out, I watched him take pictures off the wall so fast—ones I had given him in happier times—it made my head spin. I felt like a piece of used-up refuse that was no longer needed to serve his purposes. I think I had felt that way for some time.

I think he took advantage of my propensity to please and my vulnerability when we met. A truly pathological person can sniff out these lovely trusting souls, like me, from a mile away. They are looking for someone to submit to their needs and desires. I have deduced that I was good prey to control, make him look good, and supply his needs.

This is my reckoning and the truth I came to. Was this conscious on his part? It's an anguishing and controversial question for anyone in such a tumultuous, toxic relationship. I have lost much sleep reading and educating myself on the character traits and tactics of narcissists as I have tried to figure out my own situation. Waking up to my truths, as I have come to understand them, and unhealed wounds—his and mine—was a painful come-to-Jesus moment I would not wish on anyone.

TRAUMA BOND

Being a truth teller means you first must tell it to yourself. Rip off the Band-Aid of denial and wait as long as it takes before you see the truth for what it is and start to take responsibility for yourself.

With every moment of grace and every bit of learning and letting go, I saw my truth more clearly. The sunrise of my hard-won reality was allowing me to see the dangerous cracks in his character. It helped me stop devoting myself to the potential partner—the man he might be—and focus instead on the truth of the situation: the man he was. I had deeply believed in him before, but I came to see our relationship had been pure fantasy, one that I could no longer believe. At the same time, he had stopped playing the part of Don Juan.

Being a truth teller means you first must tell it to yourself.

The hardest truth was that I loved him deeply and was bonded to him in such a strong way that it felt like I was addicted to him, which is what is known in therapy as a *trauma bond*.

It took a long time for me to understand how this dynamic develops—and an even longer time to recover from it. I was working overtime to figure it all out by leaning on my faith to keep me going. I had to

Be a Truth Teller: The Challenge of Speaking Your Truth

trust my truth, my reality, with each therapist that we saw. "He has rigid defenses," they would say, agreeing with me about his personality traits.

However, they never confronted him or me. Some personalities are good at schmoozing a therapist, and his was top-notch. Several years later my pastor, also a therapist, told me not to blame myself, saying that the type of personality I had come to terms with is shrewd and can fool anybody. It was a sobering moment for me when I heard that truth.

Not until I found a PhD Christian therapist who specializes in this kind of relationship and emotional turmoil did I begin to feel vindicated for all the years of confusion and suffering I had endured. He called my then-husband out and encouraged me to move on after only a brief observation of him in counseling. At this point in our marriage Don Juan appeared hopeless and angry. This specialist had seen nothing to tell me this man was going to change, and he told me there were "character issues" and to see it for what it was. He gave me his blessing.

I thank God for this therapist who helped me cut the last cord that was keeping me with him. I had to believe in my own truth and experience, no matter what anyone else thought.

I felt if my husband could have been humbler and more vulnerable, I would have done anything for him. Sadly, when one stays so rigidly defended it is impossible to have mature communication. His daughter said our ending was inevitable, intimating that it was hard to tell her dad anything. She was very sad and worried about what would happen to her house after we broke up.

I came to believe that there is a vast difference between studying someone with a pathology and actually living with them. Uncovering your truth can be traumatic, just as mine was. However, please don't let the pain get locked away.

Do your best to learn the lessons from these experiences and receive the healing that you deserve. Your story matters. You matter. And finding a safe place to be a truth teller for yourself will begin to let in those warm rays of emotional sunshine that your weary soul so desperately needs in order to begin anew.

FOR EXPLORATION

1. What truth have you discovered, or are in the process of discovering, that may be creating deep, unhealthy stress in you?
2. How are you able to hear yourself and listen to your body to find the clarity you need?
3. Letting go and breaking through denial is hard. What do you most need right now to help you let go?

Chapter 5

AFTERSHOCKS AND SHOWING UP: ACCEPTING NUMBNESS

When you blame and criticize others,
you are avoiding some truth about yourself.

—DEEPAK CHOPRA

In my clinical practice, I have seen all kinds of grief. Often people report feeling surprised by the numbness they feel in the aftermath of traumatic events. When someone we love dies, or something significant changes or ends, we often feel numb, even if we were expecting it.

Also, depending on the circumstances of the loss, there can be shock. This is normal and necessary, in the natural process of grief, to allow our entire psyche—body, mind, and spirit—to process what has happened. Isn't that a delicate testimony to how sensitive our human condition is?

Telling clients they may be numb for a while—it's normal—is a reminder. I have seen the "progress" of this grief unraveling in many a soul I have worked with. Even within the uniqueness of every individual, there is a pattern to how grief transmutes.

> You may be numb for a while—it's normal.

Life does not stop, but it can stop us in our tracks. When this happens, how can we keep showing up? Honestly, sometimes you don't. Sometimes you just need to pull the self-care card and take a mental health day—and that is okay. Or maybe, like me, you give yourself twenty-eight days in a recovery program.

Or tragically, someone takes their own life. Life is hard. Let us not judge the one who was suffering so deeply they took their own life; they deserve only mercy and compassion. Asking for help is hard, too, but it's also brilliant. Not only is it brilliant, it is also wise.

TREATMENT AT THE RANCH

When I invited myself to check in to what I will refer to as the recovery ranch—to salvage my soul after leaving Don Juan the first time—I was faced with some seriously humbling stuff. It took a long time to make the decision to finally leave him. There were days I was so mad and frustrated with his anger and dismissive behaviors that I could have left without taking a thing and never looked back, but that is not who I am. The anguish, hopelessness, and sorrow pulsating through my broken heart at that time ached like open heart surgery without anesthesia.

I did careful research and found a place to go that felt like the best fit for me. It was a place that wove together holistic healing, Native American sweat lodges, horses, counseling, one-on-one and group counseling, all with a Christian track. I really had no clue about what I would encounter there, but checking out of daily life for some respite, care, and perspective

Aftershocks and Showing Up: Accepting Numbness

felt necessary. Don Juan said I was brave. However, I didn't feel brave. I felt like a shred of the woman I was when I first met him.

This time at the ranch was a huge expense. Being the wealthy man that he was, I was hoping Don Juan would pay the balance of what insurance wouldn't. After all, I was his "sick" wife. Instead, he said he'd split it with me.

A therapist we saw together after my return could not believe that. It would be so easy to blame him for all the inconveniences, to put it mildly, of this chapter of my life. However, I choose to own my part in the situation, and I am very proud of the work I have done.

Shortly after arriving for my twenty-eight days of "rest" in the treatment center, I began kicking and screaming to leave. But I stayed. I had shown up. I had so many humiliating experiences there, I wouldn't know where to start recounting them. The staff decided I needed to be in the female house, where relationships and love and sex addiction were the focus. Codependence was a focus there too. In our daily house meetings, we worked through the Sex and Love Addicts Anonymous book. All of this was a bit shocking to me. It was harrowing to arrive at an AA meeting one night after riding along with the other women on the ranch's bus to some little godforsaken town. I totally felt different—they were all smoking cigarettes, singing, laughing, and did not seem to be in the same pain I was in. It was extremely humbling for me. Any snobby part of me realized that we are all susceptible to the same wounds. But that was part of our required treatment. I assume it was to see other types of Twelve Step meetings.

I remember walking out of that meeting and standing outside, crying my eyes out to the woman in charge, saying I didn't belong there. It was a fifty-something's temper tantrum. But that's how it went. I had to tolerate some parts of that program to benefit from the parts that were important for me. I know AA is a great program, but I didn't have a substance or sex addiction. I had an attachment injury from childhood that made me vulnerable to men like Don Juan—causing me to fall in love hard and fast. That was my very valuable piece of learning at that ranch.

Yet listening over those twenty-eight days to some of those younger women's stories was eye-opening. My situation felt trite next to theirs, but I had to own the seriousness of my situation too. I found the individual counseling to be helpful, and the trauma treatment I received (called Brainspotting) to be intriguing. I am now certified in that amazing therapy and use it quite often in my practice.

One day at the ranch I jumped off a huge cliff—everyone did—with wires around my waist, into a long free fall. It was scary as hell. Surrendering and trusting life to catch me felt like a big leap for sure, and it was totally invigorating.

My favorite place there was peaceful and serene. I'd hide there as often as I could, sitting outside on the porch swing of the relationship house, overlooking the long grass blowing in the fields as I voraciously read books by Kelly McDaniel, Pia Melody, and others that were slowly lifting the veils from my eyes.

I learned so much about *me*, and it all made sense—even looking back to my childhood. The connections coming to me were startling. As the month wore on, I just kept showing up, tolerating the annoying parts of the treatment, and counting the days until I could leave. My sweet daughter Amy sent me a card saying *YOU GOT THIS* and I had it framed when I went home.

I'll never forget the day I left my rented home to travel to this program. I was sitting in the little living room waiting for my sweet friend to pick me up and take me to the airport. A glistening hummingbird came right up to the bay window as if it had a message. For me, the hummingbird only appears when something big is happening.

The sweet tiny whirly bird has different meanings in different ancient cultures, but generally they remind us to enjoy life and simple pleasures. They are symbols associated with endurance and perseverance that tell us to be adaptable and accept change. Native American tribes depict the little bird as a healer or spirit sent to help people. My spirit quickened when I saw that hummingbird; I'll never forget that moment. For me it was affirming that I was on the right path. Spirit is so wonderful at sending signs to us when we need direction and can be still enough to receive them.

During this time, I was hurting deeply and showing up and going through the motions as best I could. Ultimately, I had to submit to being powerless. I loved myself and my girls enough to take care of myself, even if it meant a major disruption to my life—and theirs. Life felt tattered with uncertainty, fear, and suffering, and I would have given anything to have my mother then.

Sometimes when the aftershocks are too much and you can't find the way out, you just have to surrender.

PLAYING HOUSE AND MOVING OUT TWICE!

Don Juan used to say that he liked playing house with me. At first I thought it was cute, but it soon became a truism that stung. I was about health and wellness and creating fair balance in this new blended family. He was all about his work and his kids. I pointed out to him that days would go by without him asking me how I was doing. I just got used to it, but the feeling of having no control there was maddening and compromised my nervous system and health.

The first morning I woke up in that house there were two other women in "my" kitchen, his nanny and an au pair. We worked on cutting back that help, because I said my daughter Amy, who was in nursing school and living with us, and I could take over. And we did, gradually, but eventually I ended up feeling like the invisible breakfast cook.

I smudged like crazy when we first moved in. That Native American ritual of cleansing a space or clearing past energy helped me. My stepsons really got into it, and I let them help. We laughed and played, calling it holy smoke as I breathed prayers of new beginnings into each room. Don Juan had the landscaper remove the overgrown, wild pumpkin patch from around the pool that he had planted with his kids and had rose bushes put in for me. He could be charming. I do believe he was trying to put down some new roots too.

However, the family already living there—he and his three kids—were set in their ways. The boys were five and seven when we married. His daughter and my Sarah were eleven. They had no rules in this home, and my trying to impose them and create a healthy environment for "our" kids to thrive was met with stubborn stares and indifference. In my view, you have Mom, Dad, and the kids. Mom and Dad partner together to create bedtimes, fun times, time together, and time with the children. In this home it felt like he and his kids carried on in their fun house, and Sarah and I tried to conform and get something as basic as enough sleep. It was nuts.

Don Juan worked hard, no doubt, in a very demanding career and wanted to spend every moment he could with his kids. He felt a huge injustice at not having his kids with him every night. They spent time with their mom, who had some circumstances that would not allow her to have them previously as much. It was hard for my husband to give up more time to her. I had compassion for this, and I came to sense that he may have felt guilty. He would allow the little boys to stay up to 11 p.m. or later on school nights. They would watch movies, or mess around in their room, playing, reading books, and keeping my daughter awake. Her room was next to theirs. He'd spend an hour with his daughter in her room after that.

Aftershocks and Showing Up: Accepting Numbness

I recall one of the first nights that I, his newlywed wife, spent there. I waited a while for him to come downstairs after saying goodnight to his kids, but he never came. Instead, he stayed upstairs with the boys all night, sleeping with the youngest in his bunk bed. I was really at a loss as to what to think.

He later agreed it was odd. In my opinion, he worried far too much about his kids being okay. They were truly great kids, had everything they needed, and were very loved. But none of my attempts to create more reasonable bedtimes were ever considered. His compromise was that he'd tuck me in first and then go be with the boys and do their bedtime routine.

This obviously did not make me feel cherished. In fact, with time, I began to feel very lonely. He also regularly went back to work after the kids were put to bed. Or, if he was home, he'd often get up when he thought I was asleep and go into his office until 3 a.m. The man got very little sleep.

He often intimated that the kids were too much for me. This simply wasn't true. His kids were not too much for me—*he* was. I think that projection came from his first marriage when I picked up from nanny gossip that he spent so much time away from home working when his kids were little that it overtaxed his first wife.

Early on in our marriage, I wrote him a ten-page letter expressing my struggles in the adjustments I was making and describing what kind of support I needed. I found it unread in a pile. I felt that he didn't listen well to me, so writing became another attempt to communicate. He'd ignore me when I asked him if he'd read it. He did not want to be confronted about anything that put him in an unsatisfactory light.

On another ordinary day, I asked him to talk to me and we sat on a loveseat in our bedroom, where we'd often try to talk. He literally fell asleep sitting up while the tears rolled down my face as I struggled to express myself to him.

MOVING OUT THE FIRST TIME

In the middle of the backyard garden I had created was a little statue of a solitary angel. I think she and her spirit friends were surrounding me the day at that family pool party when I told all our kids together that my Sarah and I were moving out, after six years.

This was the first time we'd move out. It got very quiet. I don't think anyone was too surprised, though I wasn't sure—they just kept eating. I guess they all had a different feeling about it. Kids are smarter and more intuitive than we adults give them credit for. I don't think I could have imagined what it would feel like to leave. I just knew my physical and emotional health were in such a frail state that it was a move for self-preservation.

I don't really remember what he said about me moving out. I don't think he fought me on it, though he did on many other things. I had told him this was going to happen. It was what I needed, and I framed it as a temporary situation. I asked him once when driving by the neighborhood of my escape, where I had just rented a little house, if he wanted to go by the house to see it. He just got quiet and ignored the question. Silent treatments were regular occurrences from him.

I do recall planning the move for when he and his kids were away and being very careful not to disturb "his" house too much. He texted me a photo of himself during that time, from his vacation, in a store trying on these wild plaid Bermuda shorts with the question "Are these grounds for divorce?" *What?* His sarcasm was disturbing.

I left him a card, thanking him and telling him I would always love him. I'm not sure why I did that. I think I am just a nice person and did it out of politeness. Plus, there were kids involved.

God bless my youngest, Sarah. She was in her senior year of high school when we moved out, and had a lot of friends and a boyfriend. She spent a lot of time with her friends and basically spoke to me only when she had to. She was just trying to be a normal teenager in an abnormal situation. I am very proud of her ability to live her own life back then. I planned for her to go to a church group with a cool married couple leading youth in their home once a week on evenings when I worked late. She went, and I think she got something out of it.

Your kids will need to go through their own grief and find a way to cope with big changes. The best you can do for them is take care of yourself so you can be as present for them as possible.

Sarah and I had some fun together during that time with her graduation and prom activities and going to New York City at Christmastime. I did my utmost to show up for her through it all. I know she will always remember the mission trip I took her and her stepsister on, to the impoverished Black Hills of South Dakota to minister to Lakota Indian youth.

The love we have for our kids can be the greatest motivator for showing up. It broke my already broken heart to tell her I was going away for almost a month when I went to that ranch; I watched her jaw drop. We had just moved into the home I rented. I knew she was very worried about me and that she would feel secure staying with her older sisters. They were all worried about what was happening to their usually joyful and capable mom.

> Your kids will need to go through their own grief
> and find a way to cope with big changes. The best
> you can do for them is take care of yourself
> so you can be as present for them as possible.

After my twenty-eight-day recovery, Don Juan offered to pick me up from the airport, but I politely declined. I felt recovered, strong, and like myself again—only better. I had a plan not to get back with him unless he did his own individual work as I continued my own.

However, the strength of my armor fell away quickly upon coming home after that ranch visit. I was still attached to him and so desperately wanted us to work. So, we bought another house and continued counseling.

MOVING OUT AGAIN

Selling his house was a big deal for Don Juan. In addition to a new house, I also got a new wedding ring. He had this thing that every time we had a big falling out or I intimated that I may not be able to stay, he would take off his wedding ring, saying it had lost its magic. By then I had given him a few wedding rings, and this time he bought me one. The first one I gave him, he lost, but he wouldn't wear any old one and I'm really not sure what he did with them. However, this time he seemed to become more distant, secretive, and hurtful in his promise of a new beginning.

I was no longer numb. After spending time at the recovery ranch, I was smarter and able to implement boundaries better. Even he noted I wasn't reacting as much. I think he realized I was not the same naive woman he may have thought I was.

In our new home, things were harder than before. We fought about everything and just could not connect. It was stressful for us both in different ways. It seemed like he pretended to care about the things that mattered to me. Over time it was more and more apparent that he was just going through the motions. I felt him pushing me away.

Shortly after we had moved into our new home, we had a trip to Italy that had been planned. On this trip to Italy we took with Amy and her husband and some other friends, he pushed me too far. Just he and I took a side trip this day and were sitting in a charming, picturesque restaurant on a hilltop when his arrogance, limited memory, and unkind words, along with his refusal to acknowledge the hurt he'd inflicted, pained me to my core. I was genuinely trying hard to connect with him and rekindle our relationship. When that didn't happen, I knew the relationship was over.

I followed my instinct as my heart fell to my stomach in that hilltop restaurant. I left him sitting there to pay the bill. Finding my way out, I sat on the steps of a piazza gazing at the people passing by through the tears that I was so sick of drying. I felt like I had been sucker-punched for the last time and was some woman adrift in a foreign movie.

This time the end was sealed. No new house, Tiffany ring, trip to Italy, or empty promise was worth the misery of what felt like such insensitive maltreatment.

It wasn't a clean break for me because of the trauma bond—the emotional bond that my brain and body were left with after that roller-coaster marriage and the emotional abuse, and the cognitive dissonance. The back-and-forth confusion in my thoughts of what had happened and how I felt would drive me to distress. Not to mention the grief that lasted for years after the incident in Italy.

After we got back from Italy, he knew I was done. He was raging angry two weeks later when I moved out for the second time. And he didn't come after me or try to stop me. He packed up Sarah's room in rapid speed. Then he handed me a legal separation to sign on the way out, saying he would pay for my movers—how efficient! I wondered if he may have had another blonde waiting in the wings. I was determined to honor the no-contact rule, but in a weak moment I would text or call him. We saw each other a few times, but it was awkward and sad.

SHOWING UP

It can take a long time to gain clarity in a complex relationship that has addictive cycles. Sarah and I moved into the city where her two big sisters were living. It was a cool place to be if you were young, with all the outdoor bars, restaurants, and gathering places. Thankfully, she thrived there.

Moving from a very exclusive home and suburb to a concrete city block was a culture shock for me, but I adapted. I made a sanctuary out of a little brick row house that even had a window box. I took one day at a time and began to appreciate the charm and history of an old city. The two little ladies who sat outside watching our block and drinking wine on hot summer nights became my friends. They even took in my Amazon deliveries so they would not be stolen.

Christen, my eldest daughter, was getting married, so I showed up as best I could through all the planning. I was so happy for her. Amy's husband, Timm, walked me down the aisle at their wedding. Don Juan, not being invited, drove a substantial distance to drop off a gift that day. He told me later he saw my daughter, the bride, from a distance. He gave them the dishes we brought back from Italy for our new house.

Amy had a precious baby girl that spring. Becoming more knit into her family as a new grandmother was so life-giving to my new beginning.

Having my girls nearby, in our various city abodes, was hugely helpful. My commute back to rich suburbia to my office was relaxing. I showed up for work and did some traveling and just lived on grace and the hope for a healthier life after loss. Work was rich with the friendship and support of a dear colleague, a thriving private practice, and a sense of purpose to get Sarah safely launched.

I cried myself to sleep many a night, and it always cleared space to face a new day. I went through some big anger too, and I remember taking the pictures of Don Juan and me and our family reunited on a beach trip and ripping them apart and throwing them in the trash. It was part of the necessary grieving process.

It's important to show up for that too.

FORMING THE DIAMOND

I have never doubted God. I know it is normal to doubt God sometimes, and I have worked with many people who have. I have felt alone and confused and spent time in my innermost cave of relentless grief, but I ran toward God, not away.

If you can get to a place in your journey where you trust in the alchemy and rewiring of your soul in dark places, it becomes necessary to mindfully tolerate the difficult feelings and circumstances. During this period, you just have to wait until you feel the new strength of your liberated character and faith. In *How to Love Yourself (and Sometimes Other People): Spiritual Advice for Modern Relationships*, authors Lodro Rinzler and Meggan Watterson discuss the Buddha. Here is some great practical advice to embrace:

> When the Buddha sat down to meditate under the Bodhi Tree 2,600 years ago, he didn't sit down to come up with a master plan to make himself different. He acknowledged that he was suffering and knew that he wanted to do something about that. He engaged in a simple meditation practice, to begin to look at that suffering. The more he looked, the more he realized, at his core, he wasn't basically messed up. He was basically good. He was basically awake. And he was not alone. We are, too. Our wakefulness is indestructible. It is like a diamond in a heap of dust. It is always there. We just need to discover it.[1]

You are that shiny jewel, just as I am. The process of clearing that dust is different for each of us. The traumas and wounds dull our senses to who we truly are. If we don't ask for help to heal and make a practical plan, we will miss out.

Currently, I am writing from a country inn in the mountains of a quaint little town. I gave myself this gift to get away and dive into writing this book. It's been a sweet time so far, doing some deep spiritual work last night after arriving. Clearing my heart and mind after the busy Christmas holiday was a much-needed refreshment. That's self-care, for me, at its finest; it's not optional.

> The traumas and wounds dull our senses to who we truly are.

Visiting the spa this morning and walking in the crisp cold was restful and invigorating. Can you create spaces of self-care, even in your home, to pamper yourself to help you show up for yourself and others?

This past year has been one of settling into my growth and sowing seeds into a new beginning, with continued healing and letting go of the remaining pain and torment. Letting go is a process that may take many times of consciously letting go, just as it took a couple of tries before I moved out for good.

The trauma bond created with Don Juan and the cognitive dissonance have both been hell to work through. This is normal with many of my clients who have been involved in crazy-making types of relationships like I was. It's no easy task some days, but I'm living proof it can be done. You have everything inside to do the same, in your own circumstances, with the right help and support—earthly and heavenly. Depending on one without the other is not complete help, in my opinion. At the integration of psychology and spirituality is where the brilliance of the diamond is revealed. Your light in real time.

That diamond had to go through some extreme stress to be formed. Diamonds are made deep within the mantle of the earth under extreme heat and pressure. We don't get to the purity and clarity of our spiritual power without being put to the fire. I love this—the diamond is light,

Aftershocks and Showing Up: Accepting Numbness

like the sun, and it is the stone of commitment and faithfulness between a husband and a wife. It symbolizes light and brilliance, unconquerable treasures, and intellectual knowledge.

I told my current husband I didn't need a diamond; instead, I wanted an aquamarine in my ring. My Reiki master told me aquamarine was a symbol of courage. And you need courage to have a third marriage.

The aquamarine also resembles the sea, and it represents exhilaration and relaxing calm. My ring to me is symbolic of my courage and it has little diamonds on the band. He picked it out himself. My Tiffany diamond given by Don Juan did not shine as it was meant to. It looked good on the outside, but inside that marriage I felt there was just too much unconscious tarnish and defensiveness to break through to even give it a chance of surviving.

For me, the numbness that was normal and necessary during the healing process has worn off. My lessons have been accomplished. I have survived the devastation of two failed marriages, and my life has been redeemed. I worked hard at it and that is what is required. My girls are happy and well, and we are all living a good life. We are close.

I am perfectly imperfect and that is enough. There is no more shame. It may sound simple, but it has not been easy. Anything you are going through can be overcome, one step at a time—with help. Just don't forget to ask.

This reminds me of an exercise we did at the holistic recovery ranch. One day they put us in this maze of ropes and told us to find our way out. I gradually saw everyone leaving, and I was desperately trying to figure it out. I was so embarrassed. What was I not seeing? What I finally realized, feeling totally exposed, was that each of them used their one question allowed, to ask for help! I didn't even think to do that.

Trust me, I ask now—and so can you.

FOR EXPLORATION

1. How are you going through the motions—perhaps afraid to uncover the truth and staying numb to a trauma or grief?
2. What helps you to show up when the aftershocks of a loss or fear are shaking you?
3. Are you ready to shine like a diamond? What can help you get there?

Chapter 6

UNDERSTANDING TRAUMA: THE GIFTS OF POST-TRAUMATIC GROWTH

Children are a great incentive and impetus for parents to learn about themselves, about each other and about life itself. Unfortunately, much of the learning may occur at their expense.

—GABOR MATÉ

We cannot be a human living on this planet without seeing, hearing about, or experiencing trauma of some type. It is part of our landscape. Some sensitive souls can't even watch the news or a violent movie because it is so dysregulating and disturbing to them. Maybe you know people like this or are one of them.

I am a highly sensitive person who has heard a great deal after years of listening to my clients in therapy. It has taken time, but I have learned how to take care of myself and separate the pain in my counseling room from my personal life. Truly, if I did not have faith in a benevolent Spirit who will one day make all things right, even if it is the day we transition to our "eternal home," nothing would make sense to me. That hope gives meaning as well as the need to accept some things as mystery.

Other people, like me, who have overcome supreme ordeals in this "earth school" can offer you assurance. It is possible to receive the grace to transform and transcend into a serene soul whose presence is so connected with Divine love that you can be used to awaken others.

However, you don't get the gifts of post-traumatic growth without integrating the overwhelm and disruption of trauma. This will take perseverance and dedication to yourself and to those who depend on you.

> You don't get the gifts of post-traumatic growth without integrating the overwhelm and disruption of trauma.

UNDERSTANDING TRAUMA

Those I have worked with in therapy often stumble over the word *trauma* when we are speaking about it as their own experience. It sounds so serious and acute. And it is, which makes it so hard to own as something that happened to them.

The intelligence of our magnificently created bodies and brains does know how to protect us, however. If you've had anything happen in your life that was too much to feel and could not be handled or integrated, your body and brain took care of it for you. The body took the parts that froze, in the fight-or-flight response, within that overactivated autonomic nervous system, and stored them deep in the brain's subcortex.

Trauma has its own sophisticated neural network. Talk therapy takes place in the prefrontal cortex of the brain, which does not have access to the frozen pieces that reside deep within the locked filing cabinet of our brain. That fragmentation is waiting for a key to unlock, release, and process it all into new freedom and power.

Often life, at a time when your experiences collide and align, brings an opportunity for the thawing process of deep trauma to begin. The possibilities are endless. I believe this is exactly what happened to me at the onset of graduate school, with energetic encounters that led to me facing my truth about my first marriage and the growth in me that was taking place. It was time to begin my work, and I had a choice to answer that call or not. While it was a difficult decision for me, I did heed the call and left a relationship I had treasured that had "expired," trusting that Spirit was moving me in the right direction.

The frozen pieces of trauma are taking up space you need for living and causing a disconnection from yourself and others; and that, I can relate to. It is tragic when frozen trauma alienates us from our true selves and others. Trauma early in life can affect the way a child's brain develops. The manifestations of this can be seen in mental illness and in physical disease. I also believe, from my own study, in the metaphysical causes of disease, and that both of my own cancer diagnoses and my mother's brain cancer can be understood, to some degree, within the dynamic of the mind-body-spirit connection when unremitting stress is present.

At the root of our discontent and distress are the energies of the feelings that want to move, be felt, and be released. This e-motion (or energy in motion) creates life-giving, inward vitality that manifests in the body, allowing us to shine with the light of well-being. In my own healing and in working with my clients, the focus to uncover and gain understanding about the distress is like cultivated detective work. Sometimes it is clear, but often it remains cloaked in mystery, and remains unknown.

Clients use words like *stuck* and *frozen* to describe their pain. The more I train in trauma recovery, the more I understand that a traumatic event is likely the root cause of their dis-ease. We can understand trauma in several ways by looking at big T traumas and little t traumas. Big T trauma is usually associated with a diagnosis of post-traumatic stress disorder (PTSD) and can be defined as directly experiencing or witnessing a serious injury, sexual violence, death, physical assault, natural disasters, severe car accident, or the horrific devastation of war, to name a few. PTSD is a one-time traumatic event with a high prevalence. "Approximately six out of every one hundred people (or 6% of the US population) will have PTSD at some point in their lives."[1] And PTSD is surprisingly underdiagnosed.

Little t traumas, although highly distressing, affect you more on a personal level and are non-life-threatening, even though you may feel like you are going crazy. These traumas can include emotional abuse, bullying, harassment, or a relationship breakup. Little t traumas that lead to Complex-PTSD (C-PTSD) are ongoing rather than a one-time event that causes PTSD. I equate C-PTSD to Chinese water torture where the dripping of water on the head or face for a prolonged period can lead to a breakdown. Emotionally, there is ongoing fear, distress, and helplessness. In both types of trauma there is also an obsessive sense that you have no control.

The repeated anguish in my marriage to Don Juan that led to my own breakdown constituted C-PTSD. This is true for many of the women, and men, I have worked with who have been involved in toxic relationships with possible pathology, by which I mean relating to mental disorders. The trauma bond, formed out of the alternating highs and lows triggering the stress hormone cortisol and the feel-good chemical dopamine, activates a strong chemical bond and unhealthy attachment. The ensuing cognitive dissonance deeply affects the brain and body and is very difficult to heal from.

Both Brainspotting and Eye Movement Desensitization and Reprocessing are effective, brain-body-connection-based therapies used to help patients recover from these tormenting symptoms.

Sandra Brown, in her well-researched book, *Women Who Love Psychopaths*, states that 90 percent of survivors of emotional abuse have symptoms of trauma and 50 percent to 75 percent have full-blown PTSD or C-PTSD.[2] Indeed, sometimes we are called to teach what we needed to learn. This is known as *purposeful pain*.

ACCEPTING CHILDHOOD TRAUMA

Prominent psychologist, physician, and author Gabor Maté shares within his trauma work that children do not get traumatized because they get hurt but because they are alone in their hurt. To me, this is a profoundly true statement. The memory of being alone when I received that call from the oncologist telling me I had cancer was symbolic of the aloneness I felt within my family growing up.

Considering the notion of nature vs. nurture seems relevant to understanding my own childhood trauma. By nature, I remember always feeling different even as a little girl. Could that have been from the attachment injury that occurred at a young age? I know my mom was very young when she had me, just twenty years old, and not prepared for the responsibility of a child. She had plenty of her own unresolved trauma from her young life, and it was made known that she struggled and was depressed in the early days of her marriage, perhaps the entire marriage. Even when she spoke of my birth, she would describe it as taking place in Auschwitz—a hospital that was not air-conditioned, on the "hottest day of the year," in which she was left alone on a gurney to tear and have a difficult birth. She would convey this in a humorous way, but I did not find it funny.

When I speak of my own daughters' births, I speak about them as miraculous and joyful. I wonder, even now as I write this, how hearing her story about my birth affected my young spirit. Mom also used to say how I would not let her hold or cuddle with me, intimating there was something wrong with me. She seemed to take it personally. Think about how you speak about your children when they are young.

I was strong-willed, I know; that is my nature. But I have come to understand how my need for nurturance was less than adequately fulfilled.

Were you seen, heard, and did you have your feelings validated enough as a child? Can you answer that from the stories that are passed down in your own family of origin? For the most part, the stories that made me feel loved came from my paternal grandmother, who spent a lot of time with me as a baby and young girl. I felt very attached to her growing up and felt her unconditional love.

There is a difference between feeling loved and being told you are loved. Disruptions in attachment, feeling chronically rejected, misunderstood, discounted, or shamed, are a few of the risk factors in the development of C-PTSD. I know I felt some of these as a child, and many clients I have worked with have too.

> There is a difference between feeling loved and being told you are loved.

Naturally, children have an innate need to securely attach to their primary caregivers to develop and thrive. If that process was disrupted, you can learn to parent yourself later in life and form a healthy attachment to yourself, which is your authenticity in full bloom. This is wonderful news.

Gabor Maté describes shame as being adaptive in his *Wisdom of Trauma* talk series.[3] It's understandable that if a child feels that something is wrong with them, or something is their fault—which is the universal theme children believe when needs go unmet—they take control and push themselves harder to make Mom or Dad happy.

This is where seeds of codependence may grow into lifelong patterns.

Original shame is the loss of connection that someone did not repair. Children who learn that performance brings the accolades and love they need often miss just learning how to be a child. Don Juan would say I needed to learn to play more, and I felt like he needed to play less! Having grandchildren, however, has brought out a whole new meaning of the joy of play now.

If the abuse is severe, as in parents who chronically push their children too hard, the children don't learn how to feel. They lose a part of themselves, and their young brains can become arrested quite early. With this type of loss, personality disorders may develop. Children whose feelings are not honored and validated are often sad and can potentially become depressed and anxious adults. Gabor Maté explains a child's depression as being adaptive and goes so far as to say that it is a major success to help you go deeper inside and not abandon yourself. As an introvert, I can relate to this; and I love his creative way of expressing these adaptations.

Children innately learn what they need to survive and how to cope with unmet needs. An adaptation that created narcissism, for example, leaves the traumatized soul full of shame, depression, and self-loathing. Subsequently, this creates harm as they project their inner darkness onto others.

My parents sometimes acted out of their own unconscious pain, and I don't remember a lot of repair work going on in my own childhood. I was left to do much of that on my own, as many are.

I remember worrying as a teenager that I had trouble feeling. Even as I write this, I question whether my memories are accurate, or if I am being too hard on my mom. I wholeheartedly believe she loved me as best she could. As for my father, I heard he used to call me Dondi and gush over me when I was little, but I don't remember that pronouncement of endearment, as it did not carry into my early memories. Maybe I was an object of enjoyment or a novelty for a time. I just remember his distance, lack of presence and guidance, and especially his anger and name-calling.

My best friend, who lived across the street from us when I was in junior high, told me she was scared to death of my father. She spent a lot of time coming in and out of my house, and when her brother was tragically killed in a car accident at the age of sixteen, the first place she came was to my house. That memory of waking up to Karen sitting in our living room crying with my mom is etched in my memory—walking out of my bedroom, my bare feet landing on the gold shag rug as I took in the long-pleated curtains opening to the early daylight of that August morning. Mom and Karen were sitting stoically in shock as she told me her brother was dead. I'm not sure if my body went numb as a normal response to the trauma or if my emotions were so frozen, I could not feel.

Sadness comes up for me writing this today. Coming to terms with the trauma you have suffered is grievous, and the grief is necessary so you can feel and heal. I have learned that traumatic memories can be unclear, and the important thing for you, in your own healing journey, is to get in touch with what is true for you—not live with a story of denial or what you wanted it to be. There are so many children in third-world countries, impoverished homes, and even in the wealthy suburbs that have unmet needs, and certainly many who have lived in harsher circumstances than mine were. However, I discourage my clients from comparing or minimizing their situation, because pain is pain. Your pain is as valid for you as mine was for me.

My sister, as all siblings do in the same family, had different relationships with my parents. She was "easier," and maybe they were just more prepared for her. She and Mom were a lot alike, but when our dad died recently, she was just as disgusted and saddened by who he was, and wasn't, as I was. The neglect and lack of guidance that we felt has also affected her life path in adverse ways. Each sibling takes on a different role in a family system. My role was the scapegoat. The blaming and shaming that was drilled deep into my sensitive nature created a gnawing hunger that left me vulnerable to making poor choices.

I remember having premonitions as a young girl that my life was going to be different—somehow distinct, with a divergent path from that of most kids' lives. It was not always a conscious thought, but it has always lived in me. Today, I feel no fear or shame about being a unique individual—I rather like it.

Celebrating the detours and darkness that I have traversed fills me with an unspeakable peace. Accepting that I am a highly sensitive person, was a strong-willed kid, and am the rarest type of personality on the Myers-Briggs personality assessment is who I came into this world to be.

Experiencing C-PTSD growing up, and in a marriage, was probably not part of God's plan for me (or for any child); but you can develop strengths, resilience, and wisdom from the trials that compensate for what was missing. The process of recognizing and admitting that I suffered abuse in my childhood and then felt the reverberations of that injury in my second marriage were burdens I have come to accept with the grace of Spirit, who is forever faithful to sustain and support me.

UNHEALED GENERATIONAL TRAUMA

PTSD and C-PTSD are complicated, with many pieces to connect in order to create a whole person in a mosaic of healing. Each person's story is unique. The way they respond to trauma and begin to unravel it is varied and depends on many factors.

Perceptions of traumatic events vary based upon the characteristics of the individual, previous losses or stressors, sociocultural influences, resilience, ability to regulate emotions, and a propensity to ask for help, to name a few.

MY MYSTICAL PATH

Dr. David Grand—the developer of the amazing Brainspotting therapy that I utilize in my practice—once said at a training class that the majority of people who need therapy will not come through our counseling doors. So, might we have a multitude trying to function with symptoms of trauma, who are needlessly and heedlessly passing them on to our children? Many researchers in trauma say yes and are helping us to understand the collective and generational far-reaching consequences of unhealed trauma.

In my work, both personal and professional, the exploration that leads to the true integrated self, to begin the necessary generational healing, is sacred work. Thomas Hübl's praiseworthy book *Healing Collective Trauma: A Process for Integrating Our Intergenerational and Cultural Wounds* offers an understanding of trauma's impact on our relationships: "Complex trauma impairs the ability to establish a stable sense of self, and therefore the relationship to the self, and hinders or severs the capacity to form healthy relationships with others." He goes on to say that "This is perhaps the most debilitating consequence of trauma."[4]

Recently, my daughter Amy said something to me that stopped me in my tracks and brought tears to my eyes. She was speaking of her dad—my first husband—the Companion archetype who was a good father to her and her sisters when they were young. Over the years as my girls have become adults, the distance between them and their dad has grown and felt emotionally void, and it has been hurtful to them.

I never asked for or needed validation as to why I could not stay married to him. Amy proceeded to tell me that she and her sisters were better off for the growth I allowed to erupt within me, all those years ago, even though it led to divorce. Facing my shadow, then, has allowed me to be joyfully present for them even through the second layer of sacred work with Don Juan.

My daughter's words affirmed for me what I already knew when I made that decision to leave the Companion. The mystical union I was connected to then nudging me forward felt holy. It felt like I was being called to take an adventurous path. One of my colleagues, a therapist who was working with me through some scary passages at that time (with a classical music guided meditation program), pointed out to me that I was on the classic hero's journey as described by the American mythologist Joseph Campbell.

I certainly did not feel like a hero at the time, with all the backlash coming at me while leaving the marriage. Now, every day I know and feel the life-giving elixir that was waiting to be found on that steep and cavernous path. It lives deep in my soul and can never be lost.

Trauma can rob a person's life of joy and trust. It can lead to depression, anxiety, separation, and wondering where you belong and to whom you belong. Seeing clients growing in awareness and clarity, even when it hurts, is amazing. Going on the hero's journey with them—into the dark abyss and shadows, then emerging into the mystical light—is an act of bravery, for both the client and the therapist. They deserve a medal of courage and to hear the entire cosmos rise in a chorus of hallelujahs. Being a witness who sends unspoken grace in the silences of therapy is a life-giving privilege.

> Seeing clients growing in awareness and clarity, even when it hurts, is amazing.

Creating an integrated state of being allows your full presence to truly be with another. Hats off to my graduate program, which felt like it was divinely anointed to help its students heal their own stuff to be able to help others. We also learned the necessity of always doing our work within the dance of helping others.

Your dedication to your own healing will create a portal for change and enable you to address the collective and generational patterns of disconnection.

HEALING TRAUMA

My contributions on healing trauma here can only begin to touch on the broad and expanding field of neuroscience research, about which trauma therapists are constantly updated. The most important piece to consider, for you, is how your distress and dis-ease are showing up and disrupting your life.

Clients come into therapy for many reasons—panic attacks and severe anxiety, relationship hardships, loneliness, losses, addictions, a dysregulated nervous system, and problems with feeling safe in the world. For example, the recent COVID-19 pandemic has brought up many dormant fears in some of my clients, which have led to a deeper healing of childhood trauma that was being triggered.

It takes a little time and deep listening as well as being attuned to and present for each unique individual. After years of practicing as a therapist, I believe a mystical sixth sense has been given to me. It feels like I am being used as a channel of Divine wisdom and grace, and it flows naturally. Or maybe it is just strong intuition? Whatever it is, I have grown to depend on it because it is usually right on. I have described it as being like an angel sitting on my shoulder, whispering into my ear what to say to or ask my client. It is a flow, an offering—like a download, and a mutual collaboration.

Developmental trauma, occurring in childhood, is often at the core of fragmentation and out of the client's conscious reach. A tool of assessment called Adverse Childhood Experiences, developed from a longitudinal study in 1996, offers clinicians a glimpse into a client's trauma history and predictive conclusions. The number of "adverse experiences" a client reports increases their chances of negative health outcomes, less thriving, and less potential for holistic mind, body, and spirit growth in life.

Tools like this, that give a beginning reference to understanding, are helpful. However, nothing takes the place, in my opinion, of listening to the unspoken body language, perspectives, and recounted story a client brings. Creating safety, trust, and using mindfulness and meditation to help the nervous system begin to relax while experiencing calm and becoming grounded is essential.

In the physiological tool of Brainspotting, we use Bio-/Bilateral Sound Healing along with the eye position chosen around the distressing body activation. This facilitates change and release within the old neural pathways of brain wiring laid down and frozen in trauma, and brings psychological benefits. Creating new insights, awareness, positive self-talk, self-love, self-compassion, and self-forgiveness are all possible as the self begins new practices discussed in therapy, fostering the growth of integrated new neural pathways.

Just last week a client returned after a powerful session of grieving and recounting the betrayals from a parent as she was Brainspotting. She attested to no longer thinking about it and telling me how she felt an open space where the old pain used to reside. Witnessing people release long-held damaged wiring through this therapy still excites and amazes me.

Our body and brain know how to heal innately, if given the right relationship and framework. A regular practice of yoga (beginning at age thirty-seven after Sarah was born to get my body back in shape) was the best supportive medicine for me as my midlife transition approached. Consider what holistic practices you may be using to help you stay in the present moment to embody and honor your whole self.

Dissociation is the essence of trauma. As you experience feeling triggered by someone's words or actions, take that as a sign to pay attention. This is unresolved trauma showing up in your stress hormones and being acted out in your defenses and emotional responses. The unhealthy alternative to embodying your whole self is dissociation and depersonalization—a literal blanking out.

I have witnessed this in my practice. Clients speak of not being in their body. At one time, this helped them avoid feeling something that was too painful. However, as they seek healing, this no longer serves them. Talk therapy is not effective in accessing such deep trauma in the brain and body. However, the client does need to be ready to recall the painful moments by discussing them so they can fully participate in the work. Therapies that access the subcortex of the brain, and somatic therapies, are effective in such cases.

One day when I was married to Don Juan and my mother-in-law was visiting, my daughter Amy alarmingly called me over to describe what she had just witnessed between Don Juan's brother and his mother. Apparently, she was screaming at him and ordering him about as he cowered. I came to understand that this was probably a common experience for Don Juan and his siblings.

My mother-in-law alluded to it herself once, saying she knew she was too hard on her oldest son, who seemed to be some sort of savant. When she would call our house to talk to my husband, he would hold the phone away from his ear, so as not to hear her going on and on about something. It later became apparent that he dismissed me like he dismissed her at times.

In that marriage, whenever I felt so provoked that I raised my voice to Don Juan, I would see him cringe and he would say, "Don't yell at me." It reminded me of something a young boy would do. I also witnessed him dissociate at times in our relationship when it was painful. I have compassion today for him in this understanding—and for myself.

POST-TRAUMATIC GROWTH

There are ways to live and manage trauma without the benefit of professional intervention; however, you must be proactive, have self-awareness

Understanding Trauma: The Gifts of Post-Traumatic Growth

about your defenses, and be able to self-reflect. The benefits of meditation or some other sort of spiritual practice can be useful here. It is risky, though, because depending on the severity of the trauma, the triggers that come can potentially cause great harm as they are unconsciously acted out.

Excavating your truth, your power, and allowing a purpose to emerge from your trauma offers so much life-giving hope to express the post-traumatic expansion into a meaningful life. Personally, because it has been my blessed experience, I hold the healing of trauma as a spiritual journey, and I also honor that others may have a different perspective and experience.

For those who have been victorious over their woundedness to gain post-traumatic growth, spiritual or otherwise, they may experience some or all of the following:

- An increased ability to relax
- A new appreciation for and awe of life
- Owning their strengths with new ones emerging
- An ability to ask for help
- A willingness to be vulnerable
- A stronger, wiser self
- Choosing healthier relationships
- Accepting life on life's terms
- Loving themselves and others more genuinely

The arduous journey to receive the gifts of post-traumatic growth is not for the timid or the faint of heart, but with spiritual grace and heroic effort the rewards can not only make your life more meaningful but also serve humanity, one healed soul at a time.

FOR EXPLORATION

1. What new awareness may be surfacing about unhealed trauma that continues to impact your life?
2. What healthy and holistic self-care practices do you have in place to help you cope with past or current stress?
3. Does some dis-ease you are experiencing hint to you that you are missing out on the fullness of a new life that may be available to you?

Chapter 7

DOING THE WORK: EMBRACING CHANGE

> Until you make the unconscious conscious,
> it will direct your life and you will call it fate.
>
> —CARL JUNG

I think I have spent most of my life wishing some people would be different. A therapist pointed out to me once, in couples counseling with Don Juan, that I wanted him to be like me! Wow, that really hit something, because it had some truth to it.

Acceptance comes through a healthy grief process, so maybe I have grieved enough to just accept others as they are—including myself. Others are who they are, and they are on their own journey. You can try, but I wouldn't recommend trying to change someone to make you feel better or get your needs met. The truth that comes with hard-won lessons is simple: Nothing changes unless you do.

I didn't want Don Juan to be a carbon copy of me, but maybe I was struggling to recover the man he led me to believe he was. That man was a lot like me, with similar values and with a depth of reliance upon Spirit.

Of course I cannot judge his spirit or anyone else's. That is God's job. But you can tell if a person is living in integrity by how their words and actions match up. Observing and becoming conscious of yourself first is important so you can see how you are doing with your own balance of words and actions.

Nothing changes unless you do.

THE RESPONSIBILITY TO HEAL

You may have had things happen to you that were not your fault. Children are the most vulnerable to being the recipient of an adult's displaced anger, abuse, and pathology, but assaults to your soul can come at any age. My story validated this, and so do stories from the many clients I have seen who are showing up and choosing to do their work.

True heroes take responsibility to heal the things that were not their fault. Often, they don't have a choice when crushing life disruptions like eating disorders, addictions, abuse, or suicide attempts take control.

I visited my first counselor after my cancer treatment at age seventeen, then again with the required sessions in graduate school, and later again with marital issues. I now have my own self-care practices and healers in place when I need them. Most therapists, if they are wise, continue doing their own work to stay clear as they help others.

My mom made a comment when I was in school doing my own inner work and self-discovery. She said, "I bet you see things better now." Seeing yourself, others, and situations with new eyes is a gain that naturally comes from your own self-reflection, especially in therapy. Whether you go by choice, from an agonizing inner eruption or initiation, or because someone made you, I believe angels sing for you. They sing, because you are participating in healing the cumulative pain in the world and they celebrate your courage.

Early in my career when working in hospice I had a client I will never forget. She was very guarded and was deeply hurting and grieving after losing her dad. I could sense she was uncomfortable, but she showed up and was reaching out for help. I felt her examining me in an extremely cautious way in our early sessions. Learning about the natural process and rhythm of grief set the tone for most of our meetings; then one day she became even more uncomfortable as she prepared to surprise me.

She had been suffering and holding a very dark secret of something that happened to her as an adult that was not her fault. She shared that she had never told anyone, and she described how her deceased father "told her" that it was okay to share with me, because I was safe. That day began years of work togethering unraveling her story and, I pray, relieving her shame and rebuilding her sense of self. She trusted me, which is a prerequisite for any healing to begin. Her sacred work, unusual as it was, initiated by her father's communication, brought me much respect for how very hard it can be to take the first step.

This has been confirmed over and over, through my twenty-plus years of being a therapist. The connection you make with a therapist, or any soul worker, is paramount. Feeling safe and at ease with an innate gut feeling that your therapist "gets" you is necessary to proceed in bringing forth all the stories, feelings, and questions. I was trained to give a person three referrals for a therapist, so they can find the one that they connect and feel safe with. This would happen if I was too full to see them or they needed the care of a particular specialist.

We are all different in our training, our specialties, and our way of understanding and intervening. Some clinicians prefer and believe in offering short-term therapy. I prefer a longer and deeper relationship with my client to get to the root of their suffering; to pull out the weeds that are choking them of the precious nutrients of self-love and self-care. Healing is subtle and cannot be rushed. Clients don't usually like to hear "it's a process." Instead, they like to ask how long it will take.

Someone who comes in ready and willing with burdensome suffering is ripe and ready to dive into their important work—they want to feel better. Working with developmental trauma—the soul trauma that happened during a child's formative and developmental years—takes time to sort out. Then there is the grief that accompanies the loss of self.

> Healing is subtle and cannot be rushed.

Dedicating yourself to making those investments of time and money to a season of healing, in my opinion, is more important than almost anything you may engage in. You matter, your life matters, and you were meant to be whole, conscious, and live in peace with yourself and others.

Clearly, this is not an easy task in our frenetically paced world. Even more reason to develop a calm nervous system and solid core self that can flourish and flow with the inescapable changes in your personal life and the collective sphere.

THE CALL FOR WHOLENESS

I hope I never forget how it felt to be so lost and broken at age seventeen. Meaning was nowhere to be found, yet I am profoundly thankful for those times of wandering without a solid foundation—and for the call that brought me home.

Finding home inside myself in my college conversion when on my cross-country trip and in the associated growing pains since then brings

Doing the Work: Embracing Change

a feeling of humility and sacred awe. Think about the last time you felt in awe or experienced a state of bliss. Was it in the harmony and exquisite soul-moving melody of a song, or looking at the innocence of a child? Did you find it in the eyes of someone you love or maybe gazing at the ocean, a canyon, or a forest? What if you felt like this most of the time, or at least you knew that as you lived out your earthly challenges you could return to that place of sacredness any time because it was born within you?

Enlightened Christians feel they are in the world but not of the world. The Buddha teaches the Noble Eightfold Path and how to overcome suffering, which leads to awakening. The Hebrew word *shalom* refers to the peace that passes understanding. A feeling of completeness, contentment, and wholeness, of being well, captures the greeting and blessing of shalom.

Holistic orientations look at the *whole* of you and me: composed of a mind, a body, and a soul or spirit. It is the apostle Paul who refers to the three aspects of man's being—his whole spirit, soul, and body. I am reminded of a verse in 1 Thessalonians 5:23–24: "Now may God himself, the God of peace, sanctify you through and through. May your whole spirit, soul and body be kept blameless at the coming of our Lord Jesus Christ. The one who calls you is faithful, and he will do it."

To be whole, each part of you must be well, connected, and operating in symphonic harmony. I have a mandala (the Sanskrit word for wholeness) exercise that I share with my clients so they can assess how well attuned to each part of themselves they are. My healing recovery program is called Soul of Healing. To me the soul is the deep place within where all the treasures of Spirit and wisdom reside—our own and Divine.

Too often, we forget to take care of parts of us. But when we take the time to consider our whole selves and get into the practice of doing so, we can get back on track. One woman I worked with declared with no hesitation, "I don't eat right!" She had Crohn's disease and was able to start being mindful and observe how her food choices affected her body. Sometimes it's a simple adjustment in your daily practice. Other times it is that pervasive, self-critical self-talk that undermines and causes such weariness. Your mindset and how you speak to yourself is the gateway to your wellness and healthy soulfulness.

You are loved more than you could possibly think or imagine. Spiritual awareness and awakening to your worth and joy require three things: your inner work and openness to Spirit, and then maintaining a strong faith. Kindness directed to yourself first is a golden key. You don't need another person to make you complete because you already are. As the young teen and adult looking for love, I didn't have this confidence or feel complete. Later the trauma of two marriages that ended harshly broke me open and forced me to go deeper into knowing myself, finding truth, and experiencing my own resilience while feeling God's miraculous healing power.

I had already been called onto the path of wholeness before the first marriage, but the work did not end there. Yes, there were some dark and scary places to navigate, but with Spirit's grace and living from my soul surrounded by the scintillating high of mystical connection, awe and trust were always there. I would find them when I sat still, cried, meditated, journaled, had a healing session, went to a yoga class, had dinner with a soul friend, or heard a song that encouraged my spirit and lifted me up.

While I felt better, I had to keep doing my work—that is the call. Achieving wholeness is a high calling, and it brings the completion of embodying your spiritual self and listening to what your soul is communicating to you. This is the channel that Divine Love speaks. Can you dare to believe that you are a spirit that was created perfectly whole and are known by Spirit?

Life's pain and traumas fragment us. Remember that when you feel disconnected from yourself or others; you may need to take time out. It may involve a meditation practice that brings insights and answers, or it may involve deeper work—or both.

IGNORING THE CALL

When I was finishing graduate school and had ended my first marriage, I bought a new car. It was black. My dear friend in my graduate program told me I was embracing my shadow. She was a close confidant and knew all the rigorous work I was putting myself through to awaken to the meaning of what was happening to me. My shadow began to surface during my "dark night of the soul" experience, a type of experience described by the Catholic priest and mystic Saint John of the Cross (and also a key moment in the hero's journey).

Coming face-to-face with my shadow parts was hell on earth. They told me I was selfish, bad, ungrateful, and inadequate when discerning the call to leave my unhealthy, soulless marriage. I'm not sure I embraced it, but I did face it on my knees many times instead of resisting it. It was glaring at me like a monster in a bad dream that I could not wake up from.

Many people seem to ignore the monster and jump through many hoops to push it away. But this never works. As I tell grieving souls, it takes more energy to resist the pain than to let that energy flow. The stuck barricades of resistance cause more division within yourself and with others.

The shadow stores all the unacceptable parts of you that you don't want anyone (or yourself) to see or own. These parts cause feelings of unworthiness and challenge maintaining the ego persona that helps you feel successful, conform, and show up in the world. Some of the ego is necessary for getting the job done, but if it is the first-string operator of your life and becomes overly inflated, it is not attractive. The origin of the word *persona* is mask, referring to the masks actors wore to depict the roles they played.

In my first marriage I was "playing" the role of the perfect mother, wife, and homemaker. I loved doing all those things, but some wounded part of me needed it to be perfect, so I could break the patterns of divorce that I came from. How cruel it felt when that mask started slipping, like it was being ripped off. The psychic energy I took holding this all together petered out—and thank God it did.

Somehow because of my Mentor's grace, still a mystery to me in some ways, I accepted the call and did not let the fear of being exposed keep me from embracing my transformative truth. Another ironic certainty is that exposure heals shame.

I teased and said that if I had stayed in that first marriage, I would have gotten fat and depressed, but it also felt right-on. Not heeding the call can have dire consequences for your health, leave your traumas unhealed, and drive you further into your shadow. What happened to me and many others in various types of eruptions can be ignored, but the pain has to go somewhere. So eventually you will be forced to face your shadow.

> Exposure heals shame.

Facing your shadow is more about embracing the suffering and grief you must feel to extract your truth and true self. Accepting the suffering is accepting that you are a wounded self—we all are; it's just a matter of degree. This spiritual path I had blindly stepped on at age nineteen was relentless. It changed everything and wanted to keep changing me and healing me.

The Divine says in Matthew 22:14 that "many are called, but few are chosen." I am not bold enough to say I was chosen. I just followed to the best of my ability, and took tough roads to keep feeling the electric, contagious energy of Spirit in my life that gave me vigor, meaning, and purpose.

As your awareness grows in making the unconscious conscious, the light begins to seep into your dreams, your soul, and your life in coincidences that make you look up at the heavens with wonder. These synchronicities are petals from heaven leading the way for you.

After my paternal grandmother died (the one who loved pink roses), pink rose petals showed up everywhere as if to say, "All is well, don't worry." I was desperate for these subtle signs to keep me going, because if you are brave enough to confront your shadow to come into the light, fear follows. However, your cheerleaders from heaven are on high alert for you.

SHADOW WORK

Carl Jung observed that his patients who managed to heal their spirit were the ones that could look their dark shadow nature right in the face. Feeling that power of awareness, connection, and freedom will cause you to soar above any earthly heartbreak or loss. It will also help you to look your naysayers right in the face while holding on to your heavenly inheritance of truth.

As a clinician who studies soul pathology—and one who is not fond of the labels—I've learned a bit about the Dark Triad of personality disorders. These include narcissism, Machiavellianism, and psychopathy. These tortured souls have an inability to have true empathic insight regarding how their negative behaviors impact others.[1] They treat people as objects and know how to manipulate others, blame them, and project their shortcomings onto others. Their lack of (or reduced) conscience causes great harm.

MY MYSTICAL PATH

For example, I wanted to help Don Juan embrace his shadow, because I was fresh off my dark night of the soul when I met him and was living in such grace, love, and possibility. How could I not share this amazing gift with the man I loved? This desire to help was born from love, but he was not my client, obviously, and had no desire to go deep into that world. Maybe he has by now—I pray so, for his sake.

I told him he had been reckless with our marriage. I don't believe it was his intention to always be this way; he just never slowed down and would not give up the bad, dark habits that caused me pain. Nor would he listen to my pleas.

Unfortunately, defending your shadow denies your wholeness. Without redeeming this light of wholeness, the channel between your head and your heart cannot open to the invincible nature of Divine Love that will help you live with sincerity and empathy, even toward yourself.

Today the anxiety from the darkness in our world cripples many with fear. But there is one thing you should know. The darkness and the suffering can be overcome by light, and fear can be overcome with love if we let go and let the Divine help us. When we do this, we gain greater awareness of ourselves, others, and what is truly needed in our world to help heal it.

I remember the day I called a Catholic priest I respected from the church I grew up in, as I was feeling weary and frightened. It was before my college-trip conversion. He told me what felt like a platitude when he said, "God does not give us anything that we can't handle." I didn't believe him at the time. But I most definitely believe it now.

There is a caveat, however: You must cooperate, just as I did, by doing your shadow work and learning that you do deserve love. If you don't know how to do this, say a prayer asking for guidance or seek out someone in a helping profession. There are many who are prepared to guide and who have become teachers and healers on this path. This heroic human journey into the light, the here and now, is our most powerful contribution to global redemption—becoming love and light in the darkness.

THE CHOICE TO GO DEEPER

I am convinced that some cannot make the choice to do their shadow work, ask for help, or tolerate the emotional pain that it takes to enter into the alchemical cave of transformation. Perhaps they will be called to do it on the other side if they are not able to do it on the earthly plane. I see this in my profession and in people I have known and loved.

When my dad died, as detached as I felt from him, I could not help but wonder where his soul was. At that time, I was meeting with a Brainspotting friend and colleague who is also a medium. I shared with her my concern because I was curious, and I had an eerie feeling. She paused, took a breath, and asked me if I wanted to know. Of course I did, and was open to hear what was coming to her.

She explained that if we took the measure of it taking him three to six months to reach the light, he was on the longer side of six months. This didn't surprise me and actually fit what I have come to believe. I don't like to call it purgatory, but more like levels of purification that are necessary to go through to be clean and clear enough to be in the presence of God. I don't know if what she shared was accurate, but it felt right to me.

Who knows where it came from, but an image of my father shoveling rocks came to me. Once when we were going to church for Christmas, he was with the family, and I said, "Please come with us." I was being hospitable and meant it. He grimaced and shook his head no, and I could sense a feeling of unworthiness that he felt. My sister talked to him about Jesus when he died, and he said he believed in Him. Only God knows someone's heart. We can feel, if we are sensitive and clear, the energy of darkness and light. My father had a dark energy around him, and it still makes me sad to think about it, especially because I loved his mom, my grandmother, so very much. His darkness broke her heart.

One day when I was younger and in my "saving the world mode," I tried to talk to him about forgiving his sister and his mother for whatever wrongs he perceived they had done to him, and he became very agitated, growling that he was not Jesus Christ. I decided to let it be. Maybe he wasn't ready.

It is widely believed that narcissists cannot change. But there is a small percentage of professionals and experts who believe they can make changes and gain insight *if* they work extremely hard in therapy and, more importantly, want to do the work. In my father's case, he didn't, nor did my first husband or my second. They were what we learned in training as "ego syntonic." They were comfortable with their behaviors, values, and feelings, and these were acceptable to their ego state. They felt no need to change. Don Juan so much as told me this. The Companion said I had changed, and this did not work for him. While I respected where they were, it did not stop me from changing, growing, and making the decisions I did.

AWAKENING

The scary thing with a narcissist or any dark personality is this: Until you get wise to the reality of them, they can come cloaked in the appearance of light, but the darkness is just waiting to come forth when triggered, and it comes in abusive behaviors. These behaviors can be esoteric and aimed right at your heart and soul. Or they can be physical, as in the case of violence. Sandra Brown, MA, a well-researched therapist in the field of darkness and recovery, shares that the public has blind spots to the Dark

Doing the Work: Embracing Change

Triad. She states that one in 100 people are without a conscience and one in five have a personality disorder.[2]

My understanding, through my study, is that such people were not bad or evil at birth, but their own trauma and pain took over. It's complex, how these personalities form. When she was dying, my grandmother asked me what she did wrong with my dad. He was the "golden child" growing up and she did everything for him, which gave him a sense of entitlement, among other things. I told her that maybe she just loved him too much. Each person with a diagnosable personality disorder deserves to have his or her unique history explored with care. I am not fond of the labels; however, for professionals they are important as they give understanding and guidance for treatment. As unique as each person's history is, the traits we find in the people with a specific disorder are surprisingly similar. These are classified as mental illnesses and are listed in the *DSM-5*. Current studies are looking at possible genetic factors as well. These individuals can cause tragic harm and, depending on the degree of darkness, can be dangerous. Some are known to be pathological liars, with the darkest among them being capable of violent, malignant crimes.

People who do seek counseling are often experiencing ego dystonic symptoms, feeling out of sync with their true selves, and suffering. These are souls that are waking up and choosing to do their work. They are ready because the unconscious is bringing things up that they need help sorting out. Midlife—a normal developmental transition—is the ideal time to begin to do your work. It is a time to really grow—or resist that growth and enter into a crisis.

My midlife transition initiated my deeper work, and I see many clients come in at the stage of development. If you ignore your natural midlife transition, which is asking you to sift through the sands of the life you've lived so far to find the truer path of your deeper choosing, the shadow grows. It can become a crisis, and you may become hard of heart. I often see childhood traumas rising to the surface during midlife. Some are aware of what is coming up and some are unsure. The forces that call us to wholeness blow strong winds of change in. Those who never seek help are defending their pain and choosing other, often unhealthy ways to self-soothe.

If you can listen to yourself and to Spirit, you can relax. My advice is to just do your best and learn to love yourself as you are becoming humbler, more vulnerable, and open enough to go deeper as life leads you. Celebrate your small wins and victories. You can learn how to care for yourself along the way and seek out what you need. Practicing sacred self-care is a gift of self-love that enlarges your spirit and can protect you from darkness as you learn to implement healthy boundaries.

Once you cross the threshold and make the decision to commit your life to a spiritual path, Spirit will help. Your character will continue to grow as the Spirit dwells within you—and more and more as you commune daily together in your devotion. Spirit takes away the desire for things not of God and intimately communicates to you in so many loving, directive, and protective ways. The paths where you can keep expanding, growing, and learning your lessons are sent with love and with a holy intention to help you reach your highest self—in order to love, serve, and shine light in the world. I have been given a passion for spiritual growth that humbles me. And I'm not going to kid you, it's not always easy.

As I end this chapter, I am reminded of St. Teresa of Avila. She was a Carmelite nun who was called to the contemplative life and is known as a prominent Spanish mystic. Her words offer us this encouragement: "The closer one approaches God, the simpler one becomes. Let nothing disturb you. Let nothing frighten you. All things pass away. God never changes. Patience obtains all things. He who has God lacks for nothing. God alone suffices."[3]

My mom used to tell us when things were hard that "this too shall pass." I love the part of her that now lives in me and allows me to embrace this sentiment too. Mom could not enter the abyss like I did; and that's okay. We all have different paths. I trust she is clothed now in her eternal home in a mystical, radiant light, devoted to truth while living in her true freedom and power.

FOR EXPLORATION

1. What does wholeness mean to you as you reflect on your own life today?
2. What led you to do your work and answer the call to wholeness?
3. What may be stirring in you if you have not begun to do your work?

Part 3

GRACE

The end of my marriage to Don Juan devastated me, and I could not see how I would recover from that. I am a woman who enjoys being in relationship rather than not, even though I love and need my alone time. A year after my separation, I met a man who felt safe and was easy to talk to. His courtly ways, gentleness, and emotional availability took me in.

My Knight is the kindest and most sensitive man I have ever known. His intelligence is captivating to me, and he can communicate factually about politics, world history, and science. In his real work, he advocates for kids on the brink of failing who have many strikes against them. His career as an educator and school principal equips him to lead his troops to support the cause of training his students and teachers for success. His work is more like a ministry to me—his dedication is selfless and noble.

I was diagnosed with breast cancer about a year after we met and he walked into my house with flowers, exuding so much care and calmness, saying, "I knew I was here for a reason." I tried pushing him away a few times, but he was not going anywhere. He has been exceedingly patient with me, as I have been with him. We both had a lion's share of grief to still get through when we met.

I am thankful for his maturity, and mine too, that helps our intimacy deepen through the growing pains. He loves me with a devotion that is exemplified in his words and actions. I feel safe, open, and receptive to his steady care. He didn't sweep me off my feet but gave me space to welcome in new life and inspiration, and for that and many reasons, I feel the gift of grace in his presence.

At this stage of life, we are grateful to be together and experience the peace and stability that the Divine Mentor knew we both needed.

We are human and not exempt from bumping up against each other's rough edges. Honestly, there have been times when both of our past relationship traumas have surfaced, and it's not always been pretty. Yet we come back together, trying to offer understanding and compassion—to each other and to ourselves. We continue to grow and honor each other and our marriage. I am grateful for his care and partnership.

It has all been challenging to accept. I never wanted to be married twice, much less three times. I have struggled with this and the complications and consequences it has had for my girls. My Knight has the same struggles with his grown children, and we have both felt shame and regret. It is only through the grace of self-forgiveness, forgiveness of those who hurt us, and a belief in redemption that all can be truly well.

Chapters 8 through 10 bring in the necessity of honoring grief and grace, and how they complement each other. I will discuss how I believe a life lived with the gift of grace has given this ordinary woman a mystical spirituality that has made me feel worthy of Love. This same grace that allows me to love myself and guide others to do the same in my work is a privilege. Through all the cavernous passages of grief that I have maneuvered, a full life has been granted.

Chapter 11 closes my story with the truth that new beginnings are possible—not perfect, or even the once-ideal dream, but simply a meaningful authentic life. The journey is not complete without scaling the heights and depths within the broader life-and-death cycle that is the expansive universal circle of life—a layered, soulful life.

Chapter 8

UNDERSTANDING GRIEF: THE VEHICLE FOR DEEP TRANSFORMATION

> Not only so, but we also glory in our sufferings, because we know that suffering produces perseverance; perseverance, character; and character, hope. And hope does not put us to shame, because God's love has been poured out into our hearts through the Holy Spirit, who has been given to us.
>
> —ROMANS 5:3–5 NIV

Grief is the vehicle for our deepest transformations and is not to be feared. There is no escaping it, and as long as life continues to change there will be grief and it is not all bad. In fact, let's get away from even labeling grief, or anything else for that matter, as good or bad.

Therein lies the problem with grief. If you can begin to embrace grief as an innate part of life with its own natural rhythm, it then becomes a season of time, a passage, and the price for having loved, and less of an intruder. Although, in our culture and in the many grieving souls I have worked with, it is not a welcome friend. The fear of grief's alarm is legitimate. It activates your defenses of avoidance and unconsciously seeks unhealthy ways of coping. Not because of grief itself, but more because of fear, disruption, setbacks, and the emotional pain that grief brings.

> Grief is the vehicle for our deepest transformations and is not to be feared.

Early in my first marriage, all I could think about was having a baby. After my first miscarriage I learned about and felt a grief that I could not have fathomed prior to this loss. Then I learned how, after my next baby, Christen, was born, how miraculous having a child is. I suffered two more miscarriages between Amy and Sarah, and with each one—in addition to the pain of losing a child, so dearly wanted—was the awareness of the grief that was unavoidable.

I clearly remember sitting under a tree outside the hospital after my doctor could not find the baby's heartbeat, saying to myself, *Oh shit, this is a real setback and is going to take a while to get over*. I was also praying to the Blessed Mother. I think she understood. It's just the way it is.

GRIEF IS PART OF LIFE

Our first protective instinct to the natural pain of grief is to flee or protect. My daughter Amy and her family experienced the tender loss of their dear family dog, Romeo, when their oldest daughter, Ava, was four. Ava loves and is intrigued by all things related to nursing and medicine, just like her momma, who is a nurse in real life. (Amy showed a propensity for a career in medicine as a young child with her old-soul compassion and desire to insert IV tubes into her baby dolls.)

Understanding Grief: The Vehicle for Deep Transformation

Romeo was failing, and it became apparent that he would not make it. Timm, my son-in-law, being the protective poppa, wanted to shield Ava from any pain. He was feeling the loss deeply too. I gently suggested that they let Ava participate and give her an early healthy lesson in saying goodbye.

Timm thanked me with relief and satisfaction after Romeo's home death because of the loving bond their family shared that was blessed with peace. Watching Ava with her play stethoscope listening to Romeo's heartbeat fading along with the vet who was supervising brought concern to this caring family about how she would deal with his end. But seeing her care for her dog's comfort was heartwarming. I was told they all did cry in their own way, which is so healthy. Timm dug a big hole in the backyard, and they planted a garden together for their Ro Ro, described as the best dog ever and more like a human.

There was grief because there had been love, and Ava did cry afterward, sometimes missing him, but she was never alone, and her wise parents found ways to help her express her feelings. She even wanted her next birthday party to have a Romeo theme! Amy talked her out of that—after some convincing, she let go of the idea. They have a new puppy now and they waited until the sting of losing Romeo had lessened: a healthy precious cycle of life witnessed through the eyes of our sweet Ava.

If only we all had such good examples and lessons around loss. There really is no way to explain to someone how many benefits and gifts come with healthy grief unless you have traversed the steep terrain. A guide can be valuable. Most of the early part of grief work is offering grief education and confirming for the bereaved that they are not going crazy.

You have to talk about it to heal. I have listened to the same story from the same client many times in helping them come to accept their next task in the grieving process. The problem is that most people run out of patience to listen and want you to get on with it.

MY MYSTICAL PATH

Author J. W. Worden describes the four tasks of grieving a soul must accomplish, in this order: to accept the reality of the loss, acknowledge the pain of loss, adjust to a new environment, and reinvest in the reality of a new life.[1] If you can make meaning out of any loss, you have accomplished much.

You and I both know people who have not been able to attain peace in any of these tasks, and that is so sad. Yet, there is hope even in the most complicated grief situations. People who have stayed the course are those I like to call "shiny people"—they glow with peace and a mysterious, knowing sparkle. They have no more fear.

Complicated grief often mirrors a complicated life where there has been trauma or unresolved grief. The fear of feeling pain becomes overwhelming because past pain is compounding the current grief. Slow, careful work processing the layers can not only lessen the current grief but can bring the light of new vigor and life into places that were lying dormant within the stuck, blocked places.

I am reminded of the lack of peace I was aware of in my mom. Even now I begin to twitch a bit, wanting to share her life as an example. She was a beautiful woman both inside and out, but she had a lack of security within herself and, as my sister once said, "She used her beauty as her currency." Her death at barely seventy-four was probably a blessing, as she did not want to grow old and did not want to become dependent on others. She loved her dogs, dressing up, and going places with her husband in their corporate life, driving in her fancy sports cars, decorating her homes, entertaining, and she loved people. She always dreamed of becoming a nurse but was unable to pursue the necessary schooling. She could not tolerate emotional pain. It looked like a glamorous life, but it took a toll. Her husband demanded a lot of her, and she had multiple back surgeries and needed pain medications to help her function. Her sister said she sold her soul for the materially rich life she had.

Once when she and my stepfather had brought their boat up to

Understanding Grief: The Vehicle for Deep Transformation

Maryland from Florida for the summer, their boat captain was walking Mom's dog in town; it was hit by a car and died. I was very fearful that Mom was going to have a breakdown. Losing this dog that she was so attached to was horrible for her. I remember thinking, *What would happen if it were my sister or I, could she cope?* Soon after, she got a new puppy.

I encouraged my mom to go to therapy over the years and so did my sister. She would go for a short time and stop when difficult childhood memories and feelings came up. This is not unusual, but I desperately wanted her to be able to find peace and full self-acceptance to heal the codependence that kept part of her locked away. I had to accept and let go of my own childhood codependence that wanted her to be happy. It was uncomfortable to be around her insecurity sometimes. Even at her funeral people commented on how much she just wanted to be loved.

Once, after she had died, I had an experience in a Guided Imagery with Music session where I felt and had visions of her in her full power and vitality. With this I knew that Mom had finally found herself fully in the love of God that was unconditionally hers.

Feeling that she now had this freedom set a part of me free to celebrate her homecoming. It made me so happy.

TYPES OF LOSS

Loss of self

The most tragic loss, in my opinion, is the loss of self. I define *self* here as the whole of who you are individually, your characteristics, attributes, gifts—both conscious and unconscious. This includes your confidence and having the full possession of your ability to grow mentally, physically, emotionally, and spiritually. If you have yourself, you can live life to the fullest and grieve to the fullest.

We alternate within the cycle of life and death many times over in a lifetime. Your young self was so very fragile and dependent on others, your primary caregivers, to reflect to you their unconditional love to allow you to form a healthy view of yourself—and to see the love of God through their eyes for just you. Parents and caregivers are human, however, so they come with their own woundedness and expectations, even sometimes projecting their own needs onto you.

For example, Don Juan was very aware that his mother wanted a doctor in the family, and he became the compliant one. I do believe this cost him part of his own self and that her demands created deep trauma in him. In my childhood, both of my parents were not present enough, or aware enough to themselves. They were not able to provide unconditional love consistently; what I have come to accept, through my own grieving, is that their lack of presence at times created emotional neglect and emotional abuse.

How do you reconcile the loss of yourself? First, you must become aware that you are lost, and this will manifest in a host of ways, many of which have previously been mentioned in this book. Recovering your true, divinely loved self is not something you can do in isolation.

As a young girl seeking love in the eyes of another, surely I was trying to find myself. When my Divine Mentor revealed spiritual love to me, I began to know true love. Expressing that love to another and to my children came very naturally.

My growing pains and growth have come through desiring to express, in the giving and receiving of human love, the intimate exchange of Eros—romantic love. To accept a human with flaws, which we all have, is nothing short of Divine. I am still learning this. And to have a healthy relationship, the other person must also be healthy enough to do the same. That requires their own relationship with their true self, and a

Understanding Grief: The Vehicle for Deep Transformation

belief in some benevolent Source greater than themselves. This is not easy, but it's so worth it, and with your perseverance and grace you can attain the love you are meant to have.

> To accept a human with flaws, which we
> all have, is nothing short of Divine.

Giving thanks for all who have truly loved you and understanding how impactful this love is—is beyond wise. Understanding your own role in loving yourself is also educated wisdom. Robert J. Wicks, in his book, *Touching the Holy*, talks about personal awareness of self, self-esteem, and being ordinary. Dr. Wicks offers an observation by Rabbi Abraham Heschel, who said few of us sense the mystery of our own presence. He continues by noting spiritual figures like Teresa of Avila and Francis of Assisi as being exceptions. "They had a real sense of self and manifested 'pure presence.' They were honest, self-confident, and had a lack of defensiveness. They allowed their personalities to be felt by others, so the impact of their presence was so wonderfully felt they were changed in the process."[2]

Ah, the energetic life-giving exchange of pure presence!

We don't get to this without doing our work. This amazing presence to have and to share with others manifests through our own losses and by having the vulnerability to be our true selves. We all experience loss, insecurity, and grief. We need each other and we are all in this together.

I told a dear friend that she will be aghast at the vulnerability I expose in this book. Her journey with vulnerability is her own. My own, with Spirit's grace, has healed my shame and set me free. This friend is the same one who offered me a new perspective when I once spoke of the shame I felt from my failed marriages. She noted a spiritual author we like who has had more marriages than I have. My friend then

Loss of a loved one

While the loss of self is tragic, the loss of a loved one is more impactful than you may realize until it happens, and it is unique for each of us. Death may be the physical ending, but divorce, an estrangement, or a major change of any kind also delivers bitter feelings of grief and loss.

The celebrations of life—weddings, births, and graduations—bring perplexing, bittersweet emotions of grief and joy. For example, when my daughter Amy got married, my first to take the leap, I could not have been happier for her. And I remember a strange melancholy visited me as I slowly realized our relationship had now changed. My little girl was a woman and a wife. When we had a wedding shower for her, Sarah (who was seventeen at the time) exclaimed, "Amy is a housewife!"

I have friends who are sending the children they have raised, with all their heart and energy expended in countless ways, off to college. This is to be celebrated as well, but these parents must also let go now.

The disenfranchised grief of infertility, addiction, the loss of a dream, or the death of an ex-partner may not be acknowledged as legitimate, but it is. It still hurts and takes you down deep into the caverns of your soul.

All grief can be transformed, so don't lose heart.

GRIEF AS A PORTAL TO CHANGE

Always remember that change = loss = grief. Allowing the flow of whatever degree of grief you are with requires your most tender self-compassion, and because it is inescapable it must be confronted sooner or later. Everyone grieves in their own way and in their own time based

Understanding Grief: The Vehicle for Deep Transformation

on their own abilities, fears, and history. You can "expedite" your grief by paying attention to it; or prolong it, causing complexities that hinder your evolution to rebirth and wholeness.

The advent of grief brings all beings to a crossroads. One path requires going through it and nurturing a healthy experience of loss. The other path resists, defends, and avoids the grief, only for it to become a heavy weight to carry. This weight carries within it depression, anxiety, and underlying sadness or anger. It is a choice.

Explaining this to clients approaching grief counseling in the first session is always necessary. I also share how grief changes you, changes relationships, and also comes as an opportunity. Can you dare to embrace that God is not punishing you and nothing that comes to you is negative? Elisabeth Kübler-Ross spoke of this. Her words here ooze with grace:

> It is an opportunity you are given to grow. That is the sole existence on the planet Earth. You will not grow if you sit in a beautiful flower garden, and somebody brings you gorgeous food on a silver platter. But you will grow if you are sick, if you are in pain, if you experience losses, and if you do not put your head in the sand, but take the pain and learn to accept it, not as a curse or punishment, but as a gift to you with a very, very specific purpose.[3]

Pain is not pathological. Living with hurt is universal and can be endured, felt, honored, and made into meaning and purpose. Suffering is the path to consciousness.

Midlife is one of my favorite stages of development to work within. These folks naturally come into counseling because they are ready developmentally. Old, unhealthy patterns and traumas that are ready to be let go of are surfacing. The new awareness and consciousness that is blossoming is so life-giving, but it may also mean letting go of something or someone. It is my story exactly with my first marriage—letting go of my dream for an intact family. When this happens, it is an opportunity for your soul to grow and place you on a whole new path. This is true for grief at any time, but in midlife the universal forces of growth are yearning to be heard.

> Midlife is one of my favorite stages
> of development to work within.

Sometimes clients require the utmost patience from their therapist. Especially when clients resist the pain of grief. I have come to understand the tenderness and creativity that are necessary to help. The grief of their anger becomes pointed right at themselves and creates negative self-talk and self-loathing. To discharge all this negativity, the old frozen pieces of the trauma that began the downward spiral must come into awareness and be processed within a new frame of loving kindness.

Many clients come to therapy ready and open. It's like they are following their heart, somehow knowing that there is a key to unlock the old files that can be replaced. They hope for a new chance of finding release from the chains that have kept them bound. They are prime candidates for the liberating work that can be done in Brainspotting—and they must allow the healthy sorrow of grief to free their lost selves.

The power of grief can make grieving souls mad, cause families to split apart over an inheritance, and allow others to see the worst in us. It can cause you to freeze with fear and dissociate the difficult feelings that are overwhelming. You can become stuck in resentment and remorse.

Grief forces you to face your own mortality and the finiteness of life. I read an excellent book in graduate school when I felt so mystified by all the changes happening in my life: *When Things Fall Apart*, by

Pema Chodron. She spoke deeply to my heart. She writes, "Sometimes we are cornered; everything falls apart and we run out of options for escape. At times like that the most profound truths seem straightforward and ordinary."[4]

This is so true!

I couldn't escape my truth any longer and there was no place to hide. I may have looked brave, but I was scared, and I was discovering that things do fall apart, and what excruciating grief felt like.

There is no greater teacher to being in the present moment than to honor the grief and feel what is true for you in the moment until it shifts to the next place. The energy is asking for an open channel to move through and do its refining work.

THE COMPLEXITY OF GRIEF

Please don't judge yourself or another when they are grieving. My mom always said that if anything happened to her, my stepdad would find someone else just like that! I felt like it was a putdown to herself and would try to reason with her, saying, "No way, Mom; you are the love of his life," but she was right.

It was astonishing how quickly he moved on after her death. She was the love of his life, and he could not bear to be alone. His grief was so dire that he did not want to go to the gravesite when they interred her ashes. I think it would have made it too real. Mom's sister was very upset by this, but I knew it was just too much for him. I didn't feel much of the pain of grief when my own father died. I had done all my grieving for the loss of a father I needed when he was alive. It happens like that sometimes.

Fearing death, your own or the death of another, is normal, but how often do you think about it? Pain, the loss of love, and the unknown are anxiety-producing. The Greek philosopher Epicurus believed our omnipresent fear of death was the root cause of misery. Are we aware of this? Is it true?

Anxiety about death has come up for clients I've worked with. It is usually associated with the death of someone close to them that drives them to face their own mortality. Bringing the subject to light demystifies it.

As a mother, and now seeing my own daughters with young children, anxiety about keeping your children safe and healthy is always, whether conscious or unconscious, the daily and gargantuan task of being a parent. The loss of a child is said to be the most arduous and anguishing to experience and integrate, and such a high calling to try to make meaning of.

Conversely, accepting the reality that you, and those you love, will die one day offers an opportunity to really live and live in the moment. Those who have lived through untimely griefs and losses understand this. Grief brings clarity to universal truths. We see people quitting jobs, traveling, and changing their course in rapid succession with the COVID-19 pandemic, reminding us that a long lifetime into advancing years is not guaranteed. Having a healthy respect for death instead of fear may allow you to live mindfully, intentionally, and with purpose. Even better, grace can help you choose gratitude, joy, and trust. Perspectives of death are different at different ages, as life experience seasons you and helps you understand the capriciousness of life.

Last Christmas, while talking to my stepdad on the phone, at the end of our conversation he stated in an unassuming tone that he had "a little bone cancer." I felt an alarm in me sound and the resulting shudders in my body. He expressed how grateful he was for all the years he had had, and said it's been a great life and that he had no regrets. He laughed in his usual infectious way, saying that if this didn't get him, old age would.

He died three months later, just shy of his ninety-fourth birthday. No one could begin to know his heart or the fear present within him at his end. Being a private person, he called all his kids by telephone to say goodbye, home hospice came in when it got bad, and his girlfriend sent me a text saying he had "sailed" a little after midnight the night he let go. He was an avid sailor in his younger years, so this was fitting indeed. My intuition tells me that he faced death head-on with acceptance and courage just like he captained his boat through the surge of a stormy sea.

GOODBYE TO MOM

Mom's transition, which came nine weeks after the shocking diagnosis of stage 4 glioblastoma brain cancer, was not as straightforward as her husband's seemed. Her brain was so affected by the cancer, at the end she was not herself. She was so confused. She took up residence in a beautiful library, filled with their books and photos, situated in the front, lower level of their home. She spent hours every day on a cozy lounge chair, usually with one of us sitting with her. We brought her, by request, her favorite Starbucks coffee and butter pecan ice cream on demand. She was very into watching a historical fiction television series and looking at bridal magazines with my daughter Amy, who was planning her wedding.

Mom didn't make the wedding but did see Amy try on her gown, which she purchased for her. With a sense of uncertainty, her words were sometimes filled with an innocence trying to sound true. One day she said to me, "Donna, I don't think I am dying. I am just very tired." I validated her fatigue and held back my tears. It had snowed overnight and when I came to see her the next day she lit up and told me that during the night she was awake watching two deer outside of the window in the falling snow. I sensed it was a very magical and spiritual moment for her.

MY MYSTICAL PATH

Because of my hospice and grief training, and maybe my faith, I felt calmer during those nine weeks, I think. Seeing my mom like this was heartbreaking, no doubt. I was very aware of my stepdad's and sister's fear, agitation, and despair, which seemed so raw on their faces. My sister and aunt had wanted Mom to have surgery, which would have been very hard on her if she survived it, and it did not offer a cure for her cancer. But if it had been successful, it would have bought her more time. My stepdad and I did not want this for her. He stated in an intolerant voice that she hated hospitals! The family was at odds, which made for some tender times of trying to honor each other.

One day Mom went about her daily routine of setting the breakfast table for her husband and he arrived to find the dog's bones on his plate. "Houston, we have a problem," my aunt said, through our laughter.

One morning we got word that an ambulance had picked her up during the night to take her to inpatient hospice. She apparently was in a great deal of pain. I still wonder whether I should have been more honest with her when she asked me where she was. Saying the word *hospice* was too hard for me and I felt protective of her. She would not settle down or stay in her hospice bed, and they would find her in other rooms and roaming around. I asked if this was normal and the male nurse, who was so good with her, said they sometimes get a live wire like her.

I wondered if her spirit was fighting for her life. She was not ready to die. The hospice medications and palliative care helped her relax and Sister Karen came in and offered the most beautiful prayer and send-off about her soon being in paradise. We took turns having alone time with her. I held her hand and told her she had been a good mom and assured her of my love and gave her permission to let go. She was in a coma, but I know she heard me and squeezed my hand and mouthed, "I love you, too." She was only there for three days.

I gave the eulogy at the funeral, and everyone said I did a good job. This meant a lot to me, especially coming from my stepdad. It is

Understanding Grief: The Vehicle for Deep Transformation

normal for everyone involved to be in shock at this early stage of death and grief and I was no exception.

At the viewing, my stepdad had a photo of her within a template cover of *Playboy* magazine sitting out for all to see. I hated it and my daughter Amy and I hid it. He screamed at me after that so harshly that I think he surprised himself. The anger was hurtful to me, but I knew better than to defend the action. He did ask why I did that, and I said it felt uncomfortable. She was my mom, and the grandmother of my children, and to him she was his beautiful and sexy wife. He let it go and it never came up again. He would write letters to my sister and me anytime a new woman or a change came, just letting us know and saying Mom would want him to be happy. He never had to do that, but he was very faithful to us after Mom's death and never forgot a birthday of ours or of one of our children.

They are both gone now, and my biological dad is, too. The men died within two months of each other. I pray for all of them and continue to speak to and feel my mom around often. I keep on my desk a beautiful photo of mom and my girls, visiting her in her Florida home when they were younger. That photo belonged to her and is in a frame that reads "cherish always." You can feel the pride and love in her eyes coming through.

After her death, something happened that I will never forget. I was in the home I shared with Don Juan, in our bedroom sitting on the bed next to my nightstand filled with books. I saw this streak of sparkle go by above my head, as fast as lightning, and I instantly looked up to see something like a trail that Tinkerbell leaves behind her in Disney movies. "Mom!" I exclaimed. I knew it was her and no one can tell me differently. I felt she was just checking on me. It left a warm feeling during an empty time.

I have no idea why as a young mom I had a deep desire and curiosity about death and dying. Before I went to graduate school and did my first internship at the hospice where my mother later died, I did the volunteer training there. The confident, caring woman with a spiritual presence who gave the training was who I wanted to be one day. And one day I did what was required to do that very training. As Dr. Wicks, the chair in my graduate program, said, it's a calling into the work we set out to do. Or maybe it was my soul and body wrestling with the possibility of dying at seventeen that set me up for such a passion to do grief work. Either way, I know a prerequisite for living a whole life is to learn how to grieve.

My ordeals with grief have changed me deeply, as they do when you give yourself fully to it. If someone calls you brave, it might just mean that you have had so much fear, you are intimately acquainted with it—so much so that death or anything that happens in your life is not all that scary. It's all going to be okay.

Honestly, I can say I am not afraid to die. When the time comes it may be different. Divine Love through my relationship to Spirit and her grace has been so faithful to me that I can only imagine what waits on the other side. Everything in me says it is going to be nothing short of indescribable joy.

FOR EXPLORATION

1. What are your perceptions about grief?
2. What experience of your own grief has had the biggest impact on you?
3. What do you fear about grief and what may help to lessen any fear?

Chapter 9

MYSTICAL GRACE: LEARNING TO TRUST

> First the grace, like a fragrant cologne, is given to us to heal ourselves. And then when we are clear enough, it flows through us like potent perfume to heal others.
>
> —CAROLINE MYSS

How do you continue to trust when the hard things in life happen? The things that stretch every cell of your brain to understand and every fiber of your soul to make peace with—those things you wrestle with through your tears on your pillowcase. People die too young, there is tragedy and trauma, marriages die, friendships grow apart, families are divided and still some trust and do not lose heart. How is this possible?

My life experience has taught me that this kind of hero-like trusting is not possible, not in my own strength. However, the encouraging words the scripture from 2 Corinthians 12:10 brings are indeed trustworthy . . . "when I am weak, I am strong." This strength, coming in as amazing grace, has nothing to do with me but everything to do with this boundless universal Divine Love, whom I call Jesus, and to whom I surrendered my life at age nineteen.

That was the beginning of my lifelong, freely surrendered relationship to flowing with the divine fire and sweetness of the gift of grace. This power of God, dripping its loving energy into the deepest recesses of my heart and soul, has awakened, healed, and offered me the deepest well of mercy and compassion over the years.

Yet in my human self on weary days when the tests come, it is normal to doubt. My first marriage ending as it did, leaving me to feel like I had no choice, challenged my trust in God to my core. And these are the places where grace whispers to remind me, and you, that the mystery of God is alive and waiting to impart such wisdom and comfort for those who seek this tangible guidance and help.

GRACE

What is grace? Why is it amazing? Surely, grace has been amazing to each of us who have encountered this supernatural help for different reasons. For John Newton, eighteenth-century Anglican clergyman and author of the popular hymn "Amazing Grace," grace was amazing because he claimed he was "wretched," "lost," and "blind" in his sin. Newton and his shipmates were caught in a colossal, frightening storm at sea. As Newton cried out for mercy, God answered, calmed the seas, and sent grace to illuminate Newton's way of life—selling humans as slaves—as something he should change. Newton made a complete 180-degree turn and become an abolitionist against slavery.

Grace can find you at your worst and entirely turn your life around, as many have testified to. Maybe you have your own unique story of how grace calmly and mysteriously entered your life, like I do. I hope so. If not, it is never too late to surrender.

Mystical Grace: Learning to Trust

*Grace can find you at your worst and
entirely turn your life around.*

My story is still a mystery to me as to why Spirit came to me at that Bible study my friend and I unexpectedly attended in Jackson Hole, Wyoming, while touring the country during college. Sure, cancer and heartbreak and my parents' divorce had taken me down hard, but I was getting back up and trying to make sense of it all.

God's mystifying ways have caused my life as well to do a 180-degree turn. I couldn't have turned back then if I tried. Sometimes I think it would have been easier to have become a contemplative monk who spent her life praying for the world in a cave. Sometimes I long to escape to that place now, but instead I do the best I can living this human life out, waiting for the day when I can be fully united with my Beloved and ask my questions to this Divinity who called me.

For now, however, the bridge I must cross every day from here into the realm my soul longs for is the prayer and the stillness found in meditation. This bridge brings me into the presence and inspiration of holy, rejuvenating grace.

It was a puzzling phenomenon to feel like God was calling me by name. Sometimes, if I am honest, I ask why, but I do my best to trust and follow; and have learned God does not discriminate. There are so many accounts of the calling coming to the ones you would least expect. It did not feel like the choice was entirely mine, but I did have a choice about how I would respond and live it out. The relief and meaning it heralded to my inner being felt ecstatic. I studied; I took up an earnest prayer life; and I began to see God in the eyes of other people, and in everything. One layer of devotion unfolded inside of me after another as I grew, and stumbled, and became less and less afraid. I learned I had been given the path to becoming conscious and whole and its foundation was living and abiding in the everlasting rivers of grace that never dried up.

This young college girl who volunteered for the suicide hotline, before my conversion, did have a purpose to help—to allow my own soul to become a channel of grace for others. It's that simple and that complicated. Healing myself then and now is a process that I, in service to God's Love and the business of making people whole, take very seriously. As we say in my profession, we have to keep doing our own work.

Being committed to a spiritual path is demanding at times. There is always a deeper layer to penetrate. Being in the world but not of it brings conflict and periods of deep longing and loneliness. Your prayer to your Higher Being (we are all one praying to the same God) initiates this sublime manifestation of power, knowing, and strength. Sometimes it's inner strength, sometimes physical strength, and sometimes it's the grace to forgive another soul who has hurt you.

Spread the joy.

Often, I feel extremely humbled and energized with power when working with a client. Having meaningful work you feel called to and gifted for is the best path for your divine potential. It doesn't matter what you do, and you don't have to make a lot of money doing it. Simply the presence and inner light that you bring to your work, your child, or the checker at the grocery store, if infused by Divine grace, plants seeds and sparks of life that can become spiritual pixie dust to awaken others. Spread the joy. It's the damn humanness that often gets in the way.

How do you show up if you are in agony or grief? I can't believe all the days I showed up at work when I was going through the continual ache, frustration, and despair while married to Don Juan. I was trying to stay afloat, love, and figure out what in the hell was going on. We all have our challenges. The point is: there is a way to overcome them. For me, on those days, it was probably a good cry, a good Starbucks, scribbling it all down in my journal, and a deep prayer asking for the grace and strength to be who others needed me to be on those workdays. I truly believe we are often weakest when we are strong. It's ironic that sometimes on those days when Spirit was working through me I did my best work.

THE MODERN MYSTIC

What does this mean? I am no saint, but could I be considered a modern-day mystic? Could you? Let's consider what being a mystic today may look like.

Because of my experience in Jackson Hole, I became a young woman who wanted to continue to experience God's spirit in my life. That seems to be a prerequisite to a mystical journey through life—to have this desire. I should caution you, however: Be careful what you pray for. The path of the mystic is not an easy one. After the awakening, get ready for the purification before you bask in the illumination of feeling connected with all beings, and all of creation. Ron Roth, PhD, in his modern mystic's guide, *The Healing Path of Prayer*, states that the experience of illumination offers us the ability to see all of life and our own human nature as energy.[1]

When this happened to me, I felt an intensity of energy rushing and circulating through my body as if it was doing its work to clear and restore my default settings. I've always referred to that as Reiki energy working to restore my well-being.

The first dark-night-of-the-soul period that I went through in my decision to leave my first marriage felt like the purification Roth described. I love the way Ron Roth explains this. He takes a positive slant, offering the understanding that God is not purging us of evil or anything that may be considered bad or sinful, but rather purifying us to receive more. Taking away so that we can receive more of God and even something better in this life is the purpose. The capacity is given through this darkness to make more progress in our union with God. I can attest that my awareness, insights, and connections during that time felt like they were coming in so rapidly. I'd go to sleep excited for what I was going to visit in my dreams. It was exciting and energizing to visit a new realm—albeit one laced with sorrow, grief, and repentance for breaking a vow I had made.

I think I trusted God when I met Don Juan, for whom I now have compassion, and I believe that my falling in love with my second husband was a form of love with a true soulmate. What a humbling experience to be led down a different path to do another level of healing, learn about my blind spots and about how the unhealed woundedness of another can inflict so much pain.

These were all, however, necessary lessons sent with love to enable my true surrender to trusting mystical love. I have learned that a mystic is so devoted to truth that they are able to enter the abyss. I've also come to believe that a true soulmate is one who breaks your heart, and stretches you to grow and heal within yourself, get closer to your wholeness and to relying on God's grace. In that perspective, I thank Don Juan for being my teacher in my mystical journey.

In her book, *Mysticism*, Christian mystic Evelyn Underhill offers this definition: "Mysticism is the art of union with Reality. A mystic is a person who has attained that union in greater or lesser degree; or who aims at and believes in such attainment."[2] This sounds like it can indeed be you and me, if we aim high, and it touches on the question about what reality is, too.

Your perspective about anything is your reality, and that may be different for your friend. My spiritual perspective has broadened so much over the forty-four years since my big conversion that sometimes

I wonder how my Christian friends would receive my mystical beliefs about some things. But truth be told, I really don't care—it is my unique journey. There are some fundamentalist Christians who I really can't relate to anymore and that's okay. The love that unites us is still there.

If you open your heart and seek the love of the Divine Mentor in your life, She can teach you what you are meant to master—if you listen. The moments of ecstasy and love you experience that fill your heart to overflowing and make you cry tears of joy, and the moments that bring you to your knees in pangs of grief, are your files of reality, and so are all the lessons available to you to learn from them. The artist, the poet, and the musician all may explain their reality differently based on how Spirit moves their soul to create a piece that can move your inner being to its most tender emotion.

I just returned from Italy, where I saw Michelangelo's *David*. Surely, Michelangelo was inspired from a Divine source. Thank God for the artist's gifts that bring our soul closer to the reality and potentiality of our ethereal senses and tangible holiness.

The loveliness of a piece of art or music reaches deep and helps us to transcend, at least for a moment, our own ego and thoughts; to experience a piece of inner resonance with the holy. That is a segue to mystical experience. Getting below our ego-driven conscious mind into the depths of ourselves and Divine love is to grasp life in a new way. You don't necessarily have to be religious to be a modern-day mystic.

It's not about following a dogma or set of rules, it's moving deeper than that into knowing you are loved more than you could ever imagine; and learning to love the Divine, others, and yourself. You become one with the Beloved and see the potential of Spirit within all things.

> You don't necessarily have to be religious
> to be a modern-day mystic.

In therapy we get to know ourselves more deeply; and as each therapist knows, the client must come to their own truth, as hard as it may be, for healing to take root. I had a young client in his early twenties who loved to come in and just look out of the beautiful window in the office. After a while he began to pause and breathe deeply while drinking in the rustling wind blowing through the trees and greenery that filled our view outside the window. He had worked hard, gained so much insight, grieved well, and now was gradually transcending it all into breath and into an awareness of Source expressing love through creation.

This can happen when you surrender. Like him, you can make room for Divine love to enter a newly opened, clear inner space that takes your breath away. This modern-day mystic had found his spirituality through the excavation of the deepest parts of himself and gained self-knowledge. Then he found the grace to overcome his fear and step into law enforcement, his higher purpose, which was a far cry from a man who dabbled with drugs and darkness. One day he brought me a stack of *Jesus Calling* meditation books to give to clients who may benefit. I felt so honored to work with him.

THE HEART OF THE MYSTIC

I am intrigued with the mystics of much earlier times like Teresa of Avila (1515–1582) and Julian of Norwich (1342–c. 1416), who had visions and experiences of direct communication from God. They fully devoted their lives and hearts to God. They were women of God who struggled, went through ongoing purification and suffering, yet they remained faithful women of prayer and trust. Teresa was called "a woman for others." She affected those she ministered to by bringing reformation and renewal. She inspired others as she traveled and founded monasteries, and her writings have imparted inspiration and lasting sacred literature, such as in her work *The Interior Castle*.

Julian is thought to have lived in seclusion and solitude as an anchoress for much of her life. Even here in her contemplative life of prayer for others she became known as a spiritual authority and people would come to her cell for "counseling." In her sacred text, *Revelations of Divine Love,* she writes of the visions of Jesus she had when she thought she was on her deathbed. She completely recovered.

It is amazing to me to consider what their inner lives were like. So different from yours and mine today trying to juggle so many "important" things in this frenetically paced world. Maybe like Mary in the Bible story of Jesus coming to visit Mary and Martha, these women chose the better part. But maybe we are not so different and could take some cues from the mystics.

What if you stopped doing so much and learned how to be still for part of your day? The apostles prayed that we would *receive* the Holy Spirit. How can you receive if your mind is never quiet? Emptying yourself must happen if you want to be filled up with the grace and love of the Divine and delight in this sweet communion.

At the very moment I am writing this, the song "Can't Live a Day" by Avalon popped into my head. I think mystics in every century can relate to this—ancient and modern ones. Where can you create your cell? I have one in my house. It also serves as my office, and a makeshift bedroom where we pull out the trundle bed for my little ones when they sleep over, and it feels sacred to me. It's filled with my treasures. My granddaughters love to come play in this space, and I hope they will always feel the love of God's spirit lingering in the air. Most every morning I sit in my blue velvet prayer chair with a candle and coffee to be still, read, listen, receive, and to intercede for others—the longer the better. I know many faith-filled believers that do some variation of this to connect with the Divine daily. All are welcome to partake. Mystical

MY MYSTICAL PATH

communion can happen anywhere at any time, but you must desire this oneness, open your heart, and be receptive.

Why bother? You may ask. *This seemingly mystical path does not fit into my life or understanding.* I once had a Presbyterian pastor ask me how to light this fire in people. Those may not have been her exact words, but I felt like she was wanting more for the people she shepherded and thought I may be able to help.

As I silently wondered why she was asking me this, all I could say to her was that they needed an experience of the Holy Spirit. That was all I knew that brought my heart and soul to this place. It was not my timing at all but Divine timing that made all things come alive. I pray my children and grandchildren will have their own experiences like I had, but I could never predict how that will happen for them, or even if it will. I will do what I can to plant the seeds, though. Had this pastor forgotten that she was not completely in control of this?

An illness, trauma, or crisis is sometimes a way the soul can awaken us and tell us we are not in charge and then set us on a spiritual journey. Others have not had a huge wakeup call and Spirit instead comes alive to them through creation, or the many seeds that were planted by family or in following a religion in church. A ray of sunshine breaking through at just the right moment or even a song that pierces through and creates an opening for Spirit to introduce its glory is all possible. God will use anything to get your attention. God is fun and wonderfully creative.

In my experience, however, it is not a religion that brings you into the mystical path; it is a personal encounter, just for you, that cannot be denied and that changes everything. Spirit is the master seed-planter that cultivates our heart space to open to growth.

I went to a New Year's retreat once with the theme from Matthew 22:14—"many are called but few are chosen." Is it not arrogant to say that you have been chosen as some special messenger of God? If you are chosen to do anything you have a choice, right?

Mystical Grace: Learning to Trust

We are all invited to become whole, to have a beloved, divine parent who has your back, to whom you can trust your life. It is really about listening, being open, curious, and desiring or needing more. When the Spirit descended into my heart, She vibrated loudly and awakened me to live this multifaceted, sparkling, symbolic interior life that brings so much joy and meaning. I decided to keep following it, maybe because I had nothing else that had the same allure—not even the husbands!

The mystics of old had infinite trust that their needs would be met. I needed to trust something. Is it our destiny when the soul becomes awakened to impact others' lives? It's an ultimate question.

I am an ordinary woman and I feel that I have been given an extraordinary gift. I aspire to live a life of love and holiness. I am not a guru or someone walking around with a visible halo on her head—far from it. Like you, I am perfectly imperfect. I just put two feet on the path long ago, try to learn my lessons along the way, and have not stepped off even in the most distressing of times.

Caroline Myss encourages one whose soul has matured into holiness, "Do not be shy about your capacity to see a problem clearly and understand its symbolic message. Be available to bring illumination into another's life but be humble about it."[3]

The maturation is like a fine wine that gets better with age. The wine innately knows its purpose, and it just does what it does naturally when within the astute care of the winemaker. As you are being sanctified on your path to wholeness, your heart begins to sense its purpose too. Grace is with you in this and there does not need to be a struggle to figure it out. Just relax, offer a prayer to be guided, and then notice what or who comes into your life.

You don't need to fight or manipulate to get what you want. The mystic of every age trusts their needs will be met. You can move through your life in a sacred way being just an ordinary person. It is a path strewn with abundant love and so much grace to assist.

MY MYSTICAL PATH

> As you are being sanctified on your path to wholeness, your heart begins to sense its purpose too.

THE POWER OF THE MYSTIC

Becoming free of your painful life attachments and unhealthy attachments to people is a call of the mystic today, and to each of us who seeks wholeness. It's what clients in therapy do. The attachments that keep you bound to the pain of the past, traumatic memories, unresolved grief, assumptions, and people who are not good for you need to be set free.

Few are called to live in a cell today. We encounter others' shadows, various forms of abuse, toxicity, and are vulnerable to becoming attached to ideals, people, even our animals, based on our needs at the time. Understanding childhood and romantic attachment styles is a book in itself. Mary Ainsworth and John Bowlby, developmental psychologists who founded the attachment theory from the 1950s, offer many explanations of how we humans become attached and how important these attachments are to our development. Attachments, according to Bowlby, are a meaningful, decisive, and integral part of our human behavior over our entire lifetime.

Think about your relationships, beginning with your parents, family, your friends, your lovers, and committed partners. How have they shaped you? Apart from being a child, have you felt safe to be dependent on them while still keeping your individual self and space? Can there really be a healthy interdependence between married people? There can be, and it's so much more than that. Carl Jung said, "The meeting of two personalities is like the contact of two chemical substances: if there is any reaction both are transformed."[4] Think about that power! It's the learning how to live it out that gets us.

On a human level, each man that I have loved or tried to love met

Mystical Grace: Learning to Trust

me at a very different stage of my emotional and spiritual development. This is not unusual if you are growing and maturing. Not everyone is on that path, though.

The professor I was attracted to in graduate school stood as an alchemical substance to challenge my soul. The timing of my soul bursting to a new awakening was affected by the energy, even though there was no relationship. There was no attachment to him, but it was important for me to figure out what he stood for and what that encounter was saying to me.

The degree to which I knew myself and was conscious about what was driving me when I met my first husband was very low. This is normal in our early twenties. I had values and good intentions to love and stay committed to him. That's the best that I could offer. I did not feel an attachment to my first husband himself, but more of an attachment to the vow of marriage and the family we were bringing up. He was hard to reach and I'm sure I was too. Meeting Don Juan at forty-nine brought a different woman, with much more self-awareness and an ability to love more deeply. My heart became very attached to his and to be honest, there is a part of me that will always love the part of him I fell in love with. The problem is if your parts, or theirs, are not integrated or willing to do the work, it blows up. One day, after my divorce from Don Juan, I was in Arizona with my girlfriend on a getaway. This Southwestern wellness center and spa had amazing offerings. I met with this healer who was so intuitive and had healing gifts handed down to him from his Native American grandparents. He knew their drumming rituals, chants, and blessings. I received a healing session with him that was transcending and powerful. It helped me release another of layer of grief and left me feeling optimistically hopeful. There were a lot of layers to get through.

I spoke to him about the heartbreak and lessons I learned from Don Juan and the attachment I felt to him that I never thought I would get over. I told him about the new man, my Knight, coming into my life and how I was feeling unsure if I could really open my heart to him the way he deserved. I loved the way he framed it for me. He said, "You can walk with Jay (my Knight), for a while." I felt so free upon hearing that that I wanted to take flight. What I have come to realize is that every love I have had has come at a different time for a different purpose. I am happy with my dear Knight. It is a love and partnership that we have grown into, and it has not always been easy but it has definitely been worth it. I can see myself growing old with him. I don't feel overly attached to him. It feels healthier from a perspective of human love. I know I will be fine, whatever happens.

I do trust in whatever my divine Beloved has for me in the future. While my spiritual attachment and relationship is a love I cannot live without, it is a higher love and so very real to me. Maybe this is what being a mystic is about. I am blessed to have had the love I have received in my marital relationships. I have given each one my very best. But even as I was experiencing the challenges of these relationships, my divine Beloved was with me, helping me navigate the path ahead, one step at a time.

The painful attachments to the wounds and demons of your past that are holding you back from the now are worth taking a good look at. How are they distracting you from living your fullest life and your purpose to love and serve with joy? Remember: The old pain takes up space inside you and keeps you from your ultimate calling to become a companion of the Divine in building the Kingdom of Love here on earth. Jesus had to withdraw to find quiet and stillness at times to listen to what his assignment was, and how to go about fulfilling it. He needed the power to complete His mission and so do you and I.

FOR EXPLORATION

1. How committed are you to healing yourself? What steps do you plan to take?
2. How does a life lived in trust that your needs would be met through a spiritual relationship appeal to you?
3. Have you felt a call in your life in any way? If so, how has it helped you define yourself and your purpose?

Chapter 10

LOVING YOURSELF: THE IMPORTANCE OF FORGIVENESS

Love your neighbor as yourself.

—MATTHEW 22:37–39 NIV

I have established that "home" is not just a physical building with shingles and windows but also an inner sanctuary where you reside. Yes, a man or woman's home is his or her castle. I love homemaking and making things warm, inviting, and cozy. If I wasn't a therapist, I've always thought I would be an interior designer, but that assignment went to my domestically talented daughter, Christen.

Instead, I became one who helps others pick out the patterns and life-giving colors that bring their interior souls to life. Sometimes we have to rip off the old, stale wallpaper and crud that is holding back the new design.

It takes honesty and love to bring in the core elements that create a solid home that can tolerate the wear and tear of life—and the rooms that are open to joy, celebration, and contented moments. A good designer makes space for it all—the inner home is indeed where true love for self abides. Celebrate you! Giving yourself credit for making the commitment to do your own inner reconstruction is a giant step toward self-love.

An important step to self-love begins with self-forgiveness and, when you are ready, forgiveness of others can come. I do believe there is truth in this. Even more true is that you cannot love another until you first know yourself, your motivations, and take care of yourself enough to be fully present. All while embracing the practices of self-compassion and humility.

> An important step to self-love begins with self-forgiveness and when you are ready, forgiveness of others can come.

As hard as I was trying to be a loving wife in my first marriage based on my faith, values, and commitment, I did not embody any of the above. Could I say my marriage failed because I didn't love myself? My first husband would probably say (in fact he did say) that I was selfish. It's a lot more complex than that. I lived with a core of shame from my childhood, for which I had no responsibility. Doing my best to suppress the handicap of shame while trying to live my ideal dream of marital bliss and raising the perfect family could not be sustained on the path I was on.

When the eruptions began, I took responsibility to seek help and understanding about this unfamiliar disquieting ache that had descended on my domestic domain. It was ambitious of me to begin grad school with three young daughters, but the desire to learn and stimulate my relatively ordinary life felt doable, one small step at a time. The career counselor I saw gave me a book called *Having It All . . . But*

Not All at Once. Isn't this the lament of many women trying to fulfill the parts of themselves that are calling to be born? It was my call to adventure that I chose to listen to over the commitment to stay in my ordinary world.

I couldn't then and can't now imagine refusing this call; and yet the backlash and losses I endured for leaving my marriage were so utterly painful. Why would you intentionally throw your life and the lives of those who love and depend on you into chaos and an ocean of grief? Was it selfish? Or was I tapping into something else? Is it possible that my need for a deeper form of love of self was the catalyst for this change? It was a change that would allow me to grow while discovering my true authentic self on this path to wholeness.

MY JOURNEY HOME TO SELF

Many women I have worked with, particularly those care-taking women who find their identity in the practice of loving and nurturing others, feel that taking care of their own needs is selfish. It can be difficult to alter those neural pathways that take you down the route of feeling selfish, but it is important to do. It is entirely possible to love yourself as you love others. However, I ask you to take a moment and reflect on what, or who, gave you the message that loving yourself was wrong. Really let it sink in and see what insights come to the surface.

Some of you may be wondering, what does loving yourself even mean? As Matthew 22:37–39 states, it's about relationship. The first relationship of love, however you experience it, is meant to be with God, the creator of the universe: "Love the Lord God with all your heart and with all your soul and with all your mind. This is the first and greatest commandment." I am so very thankful for the Love that the Divine initiated with me when I was nineteen.

MY MYSTICAL PATH

This relationship with God was my saving grace. I'd always been good at loving others, but not in a way that came from the heart of this Divine love. It was more of a codependent, false love that was trying to get my own needs met or to make me feel worthy of love.

"Loving" from a place of codependence is unhealthy because you are so locked into the feelings of the other, you don't know what you are feeling. It is impossible to take care of yourself if you don't know what you are truly feeling. You also cannot speak your truth or ask for what you need. Therapy can help with this displaced love and begin to help you turn it around to send those rays of care back to you. If your childhood needs were met adequately, you should allow yourself to feel very blessed, for you were given the fundamental developmental foundation to learn to love yourself.

Be careful, however, whenever the traumas of life come and shake your foundation and cause challenges. The challenges are meant to grow us up more. With each challenge and lesson learned, your self-love can continue to grow with grace. Over the years and through redeemed trials, the intimacy of Divine Love's mystical communication, met in myriad lovely and synchronistic ways, has caused my dependence on the Beloved to solidify. In this relationship I have felt deeply loved and cared for. A mystical parent and friend. What joy!

> The challenges are meant to grow us up more.
> With each challenge and lesson learned your
> self-love can continue to grow with grace.

If you have connected with and abide in Divine Love, you have a firm bedrock, because this Love is always there to collaborate with you toward understanding any assaults that come to test you on your path. You may go into darkness and face your ordeal, but the grace to survive is your closest ally and will take you to your next interior jewel on your journey. The layers of self-love can be found in trusting and surrendering to your Divine guide.

Find your voice and learn to speak your truth in love with humility, in all of your human encounters. This humility is not to be confused with humiliation. The truly humble do not fear what others think or say. They know whose approval really matters, and they trust that the same Source knows their heart and intentions. While it is good to have confidence in yourself, it is equally important to combine your confidence with compassion and humility; otherwise you fall into the trap of arrogance.

SPEAKING YOUR TRUTH FROM SELF-LOVE

It is so easy to jump unfairly to conclusions about others. It takes much awareness and consciousness to gain control over these unconscious processes. Making assumptions about why others do what they do is wrong, because it's the story you are telling yourself and not necessarily the other's truth or who they are. I don't get it right every time, but being conscious to not make assumptions by understanding and listening is prudent. People will surprise us.

Reading *The Four Agreements* by Don Miguel Ruiz was life-changing to me and I often suggest it for my clients to read. When I visited the recovery ranch after my breakdown from leaving Don Juan, this cathartic book was given to all the patients to read. It can be said in many ways—and perhaps the words of Jesus from Mark 7:2 are our finest example: "He tells us that in the same way you judge others, you will be judged." Mom used to say, "Don't judge another until you have walked in their moccasins."

New Christians, in my opinion, are very good at judging. I fit well in that category as a younger Christian. You can feel so empowered with your new convictions and understandings that it comes off assbackwards. New therapists are guilty of this too—maybe this happens to many professionals who find themselves experiencing a new source of power within themselves. Early on in the relationship, Don Juan's nanny once shared with me how cocky he was as a new doctor in the office she worked in with him. I didn't believe her at the time, but as his mask dropped there was no doubt that he had this trait. Someone can look humble and put on a persona of humility until they feel perceived criticism, a boundary is implemented, or they are held accountable; and then their true self comes out. For example, rage can live under a persona of humility if a self-image is threatened. If this happens, you witness a narcissistic injury.

Is there a difference in knowing someone well and calling them out on their bullshit and judging them? Or, in a milder way, letting them know how and when they have hurt you?

I could have never done either back before my long journey home to myself. I did not even have a voice or know what speaking my truth meant. Can you speak your truth in a loving way while taking the risk to share your feelings with another? Absolutely yes. This may be the best test of loving yourself, and it will take practice. They may not hear you though, and worse, they may turn it around on you and make you feel like you are the one with the problem.

After wrestling with the character of Don Juan and trying to figure him out, I learned so much about trusting myself. This is another jewel of self-love. It takes courage and discernment to decide when to speak up, which is very different from judgment. Communicating from the heart to someone you care about takes careful insight and intuition.

I have no tolerance for subtle digs launched my way anymore—be they conscious or unconscious. I have been hurt over the years with indirect slights, and I felt I couldn't respond. I just took it and shook it off, somehow always giving others the benefit of the doubt. No

Loving Yourself: The Importance of Forgiveness

more will or can I do that if something feels wrong and my body's wisdom confirms it. I can, and so can anyone, feel anger or an emotional hurt in the body. We just need to be attuned and pay attention to the body's messages—the quickening heartbeat, the tense muscles, the breath changing. Many in therapy begin to feel more of their emotional self as they heal and do their work. The energy centers, known as chakras, open and this vital life energy begins to flow freely. This concept of the chakra system originated in India over four thousand years ago, and came to the West through the practice of yoga.[1]

We can develop blocks in certain areas of our bodies where these chakras reside, through traumas and unresolved hurts. For example, a client who has trouble speaking their truth or has unexpressed emotions may feel discomfort in the throat chakra area of their body. This often happens during a Brainspotting session, as the body and brain are working innately to heal. As I have practiced yoga over these years, meditated, and healed my own wounds, I, like many clients, embrace a new feeling of healthy empowerment.

Now, I will feel no grudge, no lost sleep—only the courage it takes to implement a boundary when necessary. When this boundary comes from a place of self-love and self-care by trusting in your own perception, you have begun to be a true friend to yourself. Changes in friendships are inevitable. Cherishing the ones you can feel safe with and not judged by is priceless. Trust your intuition. You will know when these special relationships exist.

Many of the women—and some men—I work with are recovering from the devastating effects of emotional abuse in a marital or family relationship. This abuse can be so covert and subtle that it makes your head spin, causing tremendous self-doubt, confusion, and even illness. This gaslighting behavior must be learned about so the abuser can be confronted—and you can protect yourself. Start to notice the way people make you feel.

For example, my father, who was emotionally abusive, made me feel scared, sad, and troublesome. My wounded self internalized the message that I was inadequate, and it was an absolutely awful feeling to grow up with. He often seemed annoyed with me, or just my presence. His favorite degrading term for me was "ungrateful brat." He seemed to feel entitled to respect. I remember being slapped across the face by him and he wore a big ring. I learned not to upset him as he was prone to big anger. I never really confronted him, except in my rebellion as a teen.

Over the years I tried to get him to love me and wanted desperately for him to act like a real, caring, and devoted father. When I was getting married for the first time and after my girls were born, I tried to get close to him. We had some good times then, but it never stayed consistent. He always seemed to do something hurtful to cause division. Like the time he prided himself as the hero grandfather for buying Amy a pony, and then turned around and sold it when offered a lot of money for it. It was heartbreaking to my young daughter.

Eventually, I grieved the loss of not having the type of relationship with him that I wanted. I detached from trying for the last time, after a very harsh and abusive phone call, when I was single after my second marriage ended. He was getting older (in his eighties) and was alone, with little to call his own. He didn't like that I would not give him money, so the rage let loose. I don't know if he wanted the money to gamble or for food or rent. I never asked.

I do believe that my spiritual Father, who sees every tear, righted these wrongs by drawing me to His heart of grace. Through this love alone you can begin to love, value, and have compassion for yourself—even the young part of you that was abused. It may take time and you may need to learn some hard lessons, including how to not let others define you; but once you learn, you will feel free and walk with dignity.

Loving Yourself: The Importance of Forgiveness

Feeling empowered, as mentioned, is a description many survivors of emotional abuse express when they finally stand up to their insidious abusers. To hear the many voices of the brave fledgling true selves I have worked with, echoing their hallelujahs as they break free from the oppression of power and control, is glorious.

My own uphill journey of overcoming several types of narcissism leads the charge for them. I was aghast when I picked up an illuminating book at the recovery ranch that defined gaslighting with examples that were all too familiar in my second marriage. The irony, and red flag to be understood, is that someone with narcissistic traits who seems very natural at being charming and seductive may also be capable of being passive-aggressive, cunning, and manipulative. Coming up against a gaslighter is one of the most unbelievably mind-blowing ordeals a heart can endure. Yet, it can also be the suffering in this experience that refines you into a deeper version of your true self, like all the facets of a diamond shining as it comes into the light.

Darlene Lancer, MFT, states that when awakening to the reality that you are with a disordered person, you may feel guilty for doubting the person you've come to trust. Learn to identify the behavior patterns and get the support and validation you need to become clear. Then accept, if necessary, that this hurtful person in your life may have serious character disturbances. I have had someone I love look me straight in the eye and tell me, many times, that I said something I know I did not. It was more than maddening, especially when I was then told I must be losing my mind.

The subtle effects of gaslighting are very damaging, especially in a relationship built on trust and love. Gaslighting damages self-confidence and trust in yourself and causes you to question your own reality. The effort and hard work you do to first identify this and then take the actions needed to separate yourself from it are nothing short of self-love.

MY MYSTICAL PATH

THE GROWTH OF SELF-LOVE

You were created and brought into this world with parents and family who hopefully delighted in your arrival and presence. These soul guardians took on a massive responsibility to care for you. The physical care of feeding, clothing, and giving you a warm place to thrive was only a part of it though. Thriving comes also from how they mirrored you.

How did your mother, for example, mirror you? By validating your emotions, feelings, and behavior? By responding to your needs? As a young child, did you feel your self-worth grow, or did it instead become distorted? Whichever the case, it took place through the mirroring eyes of how those primary caregivers were able to see, hear, and accurately mirror, in their caretaking, what was delighting you or causing you distress. In this ideal interaction you learn that you matter, you are loved, and are lovely in their sight. In this way, your self-esteem, confidence, and natural gifts can be developed with continuing care and connection.

Conversely, a nonresponsive caregiver sends a child the opposite messages, such as: "I should feel guilty for having needs"; "I am bad"; "I can't rely on my feelings"; "My impulses can't be trusted"; or "I am not worthy of love." This symbiosis is recorded in the developing brain from day one.

I have this memory of a birthday. I remember my mom setting up a party atmosphere around the dining room table and I am not sure how old I was, maybe thirteen. I had not really taken up any hobbies at this time except learning how to twirl a baton. My friend's family had found the baton-twirling class and shared it with mine. We twirled in local parades and were called the High Steppers. My grandmother sewed my uniforms with such care. Sewing was her hobby, and I think she really enjoyed making those uniforms.

I don't remember if both my parents were at my party, but I've seen an old photo with Mom holding a cake. I was presented with a sewing machine for my gift while sitting at the head of the table. I wept. I distinctly remember the feeling of being seen, and I think it was so rare and inconsistent an experience in my psyche that I was overwhelmed. It was not the sewing machine. It was a connection that showed that someone, probably Mom, knew me and saw a gift or desire in me to create. It was as if to say, "You can do this." There was some felt love in that moment, but it was not enough to keep me from looking for love and validation outside of myself.

As I mentioned early on, you are not responsible for what family or circumstance you came into the world to survive in. And sadly, for some, learning unhealthy coping mechanisms and patterns is a means of survival. Therapists see clients every day with developmental trauma. Just yesterday I was with a young man approaching midlife, discussing with incredible courage the tone of the music that played frequently in his home. He described the constant arguing between his parents, and the lack of guidance he received as both parents lived in their own worlds and did their own thing. His dad was working on his PhD when he was growing up, "but it wasn't that bad," he said.

This is common. I often hear a client feel guilty for "exposing" their parents. But what about the severe consequences the lack of mirroring and guidance have cost this young man, who dove into drugs and is now having to process all the shame and guilt he carries while working through recovery?

I have come to realize, after hearing so many stories with similar themes, that parenting our children well is the highest calling. Otherwise, the child of the ill-equipped parent is left to clean up the rubbish and wreckage done to them. Growing up is hard enough. We need a tribe who loves and sees us. I was one of these lost souls, so my heart knows this experience well.

MY MYSTICAL PATH

> I have come to realize, after hearing so many stories with similar themes, that parenting our children well is the highest calling.

I hope the genuine empathy I offer my clients can offer an alternative mirror to each one of them. When clients offer me their gratitude and walk out of the door saying, "I appreciate you," I know I am in the right place.

Rebuilding around your wounded parts and cultivating self-love can happen in so many ways, regardless of how your parents did. Communities reflecting your worth are valuable and healing. Some of my clients find this in Twelve Step groups, or in church groups like Celebrate Recovery. All of the Twelve Step Anonymous groups (AA, NA, SLAA, CODA, etc.) give an alternate and second chance to be mirrored and fully received. In doing the work to correct a distorted self-concept, self-love will begin to be restored as you learn to parent yourself. Hallelujah.

Working through the wounds and psychological principles of human development and repairing the self-concept through trauma work is one aspect to healing and loving the self. Yet, there is another, more radical way. The transcendent mystery and movement of Spirit—the inner way—offers infinite possibilities to experience love. The mirror of God's unconditional love for you breaks through the isolation, alienation, and shame in a flash of resonance in which you know where and to whom you belong.

Today in the growth of the mind, body, spirit, and mindfulness movement, people are practicing yoga, filling meditation classes, and reconnecting with nature as a way to return to their Source of connection and experience a transcendence that allows peace and stillness to be deeply felt. I find this very exciting. My granddaughter Ava has a little affirmation song she learned in kindergarten that is fantastic!

COMING HOME

This inner path, this mystical path to waking up to the oneness of all creation, leads you "home." As a woman who has grown up through many tests and growing pains and feels herself to have "been made" finally into a solid self—I can say I have true self-love.

Oh, how I long to be thirty again and have then the self-love and grounded confidence that I feel now; but it doesn't always work like that. Begin with self-compassion. The work of psychologist Kristen Neff is a good place to begin that offers self-compassion teaching. This practice will help you to awaken self-love if you have a deficit. Don't give up and don't be afraid; the Divine Love of the Mentor, the Divine Counselor, is listening for your prayer of surrender.

The Love may come via illness, losing a job, or divorce. Regardless of the form it takes, dare to trust and find those who are called to help guide you, just as my clients have done with me.

Your self-love is waiting to be born and nurtured in you, and later in life is the best time to do that. In therapy, as an adult, you can learn how to become your own parent. It's a choice that needs your commitment and a willingness to learn how to care for yourself. You were born innocent and true, and your highest self already resides within you. It carefully needs to be awakened and nurtured within the deepest part of you to grow, blossom, and exude the love you were meant to know and share.

This is the essence of becoming who you were created to be. It can feel like a solitary journey at times. And sometimes it is. Regardless of how alone you feel, learn to love your own company and learn to find the ones you can begin to be vulnerable with.

Self-love also involves forgiving yourself. This is often the hardest for many, as it was for me. Sometimes we act unconsciously out of our wounded feelings. I told this to a very sensitive client when he spoke of deep guilt around normal developmental behaviors; he had acted out as a child and adolescent. Perhaps it was helpful to tell him that his behaviors were not uncommon for kids growing up and exploring their sexuality.

But simply validating and empathizing with his pain and guilt may have been even more helpful. Beyond that, if he can come to embrace God's mercy, grace, and compassion for himself he will be truly liberated from his shame, but that is between him and God. Therapists can only plant the seeds.

FORGIVENESS AND SELF-LOVE

The pain of leaving my first marriage not only summoned my desire for God's forgiveness and understanding, which I (amazingly) felt I received, but it also required that I forgive myself. As previously stated, I was conscious that I had what I needed, through that same love, and that as a mom I could help my girls through their own grief. Forgiving myself took time, continued prayer, and learning to be kind to myself.

I had done the best I could and that was all I could give. I found grace to trust that the years of coming to my truth and taking the actions needed for that separation were behind me now, as I moved forward. I felt carried through that time somehow.

In forgiving myself with Don Juan, I had to come to terms with a similar story in very different circumstances. I had to see the man I loved as wounded and unwilling to do his own work. I had to own how vulnerable I was, and the blind spot I had when I married him. I had to take responsibility for all the pain my girls and I endured. It was much harder. I felt like I had willingly participated in creating an irreparable mess.

Don Juan, with his odd sense of humor, once said to me that I must feel like a victim in a drive-by shooting. He knew I was in over my head with him and the life I said yes to. If you search your soul and can honestly say that you gave it—whatever *it* is—everything you could and loved as well as you knew how, you make room for self-forgiveness and self-respect. If I did not feel as loved by God as I can humbly say that I do, it would have been a different path through—if I ever made it through.

Forgiving another is not believing that the hurt inflicted on you was right or okay. The act of offering mercy and grace to another, or just putting it into God's capable hands, is a mystical act of letting your ego surrender the feelings of entitlement to do justice or have vengeance.

The act of forgiving by grace becomes your transformational act to be love, which includes loving yourself. Forgiving Don Juan took a deep understanding of his limitations, which allowed my spirit to begin to release the bittersweet memories and need for closure that the stronghold of the trauma bond had tormented me with for many years.

> The act of forgiving by grace becomes your transformational act to be love, which includes loving yourself.

FOR EXPLORATION

1. What is your perspective and experience of self-love?
2. In what ways do you feel like you have "come home" to yourself? If you don't feel you have, how might you begin?
3. How does self-forgiveness speak to you? How about forgiveness of another?

Chapter 11

CREATING YOUR MEANINGFUL LIFE: INVITING PEACE

> I slept and dreamt that life was joy. I awoke and saw that life was service. I acted and behold, service was joy.
>
> —RABINDRANATH TAGORE

There is abundant research—from positive psychology to deep ancient spiritual texts and world religions—describing the convictions and experiences that bring us meaning. My wish is not to deluge you with the findings of others but rather to share with you what has brought meaning to me—in the hope that you will find parallels that plant seeds of meaning or curiosity in your own life.

Ultimately, peace comes from accepting your path just as it is, and this will take the integration of grief, any trauma, your shadow, and the guts to do your hard work. Therein is the glory of the work.

My Don Juan used to utter a sweet prayer while dining. He would kiss my hand and say, "Thank you for this moment of happiness."

While our relationship did not last, there were special moments like these that drew me to this part of his soul. For happiness is what we find in the moment, and his gratitude for that filled me with such appreciation in those shared moments.

Peace comes from accepting your path just as it is.

THE HERO'S JOURNEY

I've been married three times, have overcome emotional abuse, and survived cancer twice. I've experienced depths of grace that not everyone gets to immerse themselves in until they die. I did die metaphorically, however, since each marriage that ended was a sort of death. It was a metamorphosis, fraught with heart-wrenching come-to-Jesus questions and losses and then—only then—after the painful seemingly never-ending grief, it came. As slowly and certainly as the years gone by sneak up on us—the resurrection of a new me surfaced.

There is no glory without guts and surrender. Maybe this is why believers in His death, including me, love Jesus so much. We are one with Him in our suffering and in our rising.

Actually, we are all "one" no matter what we believe. One in this earthly cacophony of life, finding what meaning to believe in to bring us home—eternally and to ourselves. During those "deaths," imagining my bleeding heart intertwined with Jesus on that cross allowed meaning and belonging to enter, and I was unequivocally not alone. Grace is supernatural. It is a superpower that I and others have that is gifted to us. I can take no credit for it.

Once I experienced this level of grace there was no going back. It fills this body I am living in, the empty surrendered vessel, with resurrected energy. Grace is life-giving to me, and from me to those I love,

Creating Your Meaningful Life: Inviting Peace

serve, and care for. Finding meaning for yourself matters. How else can you make sense of this capricious life? What would your answer be to the question "What have I been created for and what I am to do with this life I have been given?"

Feeling the Spirit penetrating my heart and body that night at the Rocky Mountain Ministry, when some unknown part of me was searching and longing for some manifestation of hope, was a very significant day. There was a gift delivered in biblical truths with corresponding values and a path was laid out that I could believe in. A paved path with holes to fall into and mountaintops to sing on top of, all intertwining along the unexplored road. The map to follow had detours of free choice and free will along the way—yet another gift from my Beloved Mentor.

Like Dorothy in *The Wizard of Oz*, I followed as best I could with the companions I found along the way. But it was not in the way I imagined it. The pastor of my church at the time said a word to me with deep feeling, looking me right in the eye, that rainy blustery evening in my city row house. The aroma of fresh-baked lasagna and spices floated in the air. I wanted all my kids there to pray with me and to witness the power of prayer, so I had prepared a homemade dinner for us to enjoy after the prayers were offered. I needed them around me. The church family had come to pray for me before my breast cancer surgery, and the pastor said, "We ask why, why, do these things happen . . . but this is your path."

I accept and I surrender. I've been here before. I accept it all, and in that I am truly free. It's the path that has become meaningful for me. It will take me where I'm meant to go or to what I need to learn. God will use it, or I will die from the cancer. Either way that will be my path.

We all have a path. To try and predict what land mines will be on that path is impossible. Maybe there will be none. Maybe eruptions of growth will change your direction. There may even be a death. Each path has as much meaning as we give it. As Proverbs 16:9 says, "We can make our plans, but the Lord determines our steps."

But is our life plan predestined? Did we choose the life we are living? Were we reincarnated to live this life to evolve our soul? My beliefs have changed over the years since my nineteen-year-old soul accepted Christ into her life. The foundation is the same, but the windows looking out have created openings for a God and a Love that is bigger than I once imagined. People of faith can argue, we can believe we are right and others are wrong. Again, I don't put God in a box anymore. The Divine is Love, and there is also room for some mystery.

I know this can be challenging, this not knowing. But I encourage you to embrace the mystery on your path. By doing so, you open yourself up to even greater depths than you may have already imagined. It just takes that initial leap of faith. I am grateful to share what I have learned to those who are crossing the divides of their own search for meaning as they walk their path. Maybe you have something to offer another, in your own life experience, that will plant a seed in their quest for spiritual connection.

MEETING ALLIES

I met a kind, white-bearded professor while finishing my undergraduate degree. He was a Jungian analyst who offered me my first glimpse into this depth of psychoanalysis whose theories I base some of my own practice of therapy on today. During my independent studies with him, we discussed faith, philosophy, and life in ways that took God out of a box. At that time, I felt safer keeping God in my box.

Artwork and strange artifacts hung from the ceiling and photos popped out from the piles of books taking up entire walls in his small office. My eyes took in every detail. Every stone, drawing, and statue

Creating Your Meaningful Life: Inviting Peace

seemed alive and radiated with profound meaning and symbolism, like treasures in a museum.

Being there felt simultaneously rich and intriguing. He was filled with light and never challenged the fundamental beliefs I held then. His wisdom must have told him that I was young on my path of enlightenment, and he respected where I was. "There will always be people who have more than you and people who have less than you," he shared with me one day. At the time I thought he meant material things, but now I wonder if he meant depth, understanding, or wisdom—or maybe all three. Either way, he was right.

As a therapist in grad school once told me, "Some are just a little farther along the path than others." At the time I wondered how this applied to me when my first marriage was feeling so dead and I was at a major crossroads. I just knew I had stepped on the path that there was no turning back from. As previously stated, often this path comes in midlife, as it did for me.

I came across a lovely book during that midlife anguish that normalized what was churning in me. I learned what I was experiencing was a purposeful transition, not a crisis—an opportunity to mature and grow on a spiritual path! Oh, how I loved and treasured this book. *Dear Heart, Come Home: The Path of Midlife Spirituality* by Joyce Rupp states, "Carl Jung termed the process of uniting the opposites within us as 'individuation.' It is how we become our true or authentic selves. During the first half of life, we developed one portion of who we are. Midlife challenges us to discover and to own the other side or other aspects of who we are."[1] Rupp also states that if we do not take the time for this deeper examination, the second half of life may become stagnant and dull.

My life has been anything but dull since making the excruciatingly hard decision to leave my first marriage. The true love I thought I'd found in Don Juan shook me to my core and tested all the work I had done. I've had moments like at the wedding of my daughter Amy—the first to get married—when I ached for the intact family I had worked so hard to establish with my first husband, the Companion. I felt a wave of shame telling me I was inadequate. It was a fleeting, painful feeling, which I have come to accept can be triggered on rare occasions, and it happened during the service where commitment and vows were being made.

With grace, my greatest ally, I once again understood why I could not stay in my first marriage. Losses like these may feel acute at times like this, but if you look at these times as part of the complete whole of your Divine plan or path, you may take some comfort in accepting this is how things were supposed to unfold for you.

I am so very thankful for the allies that came to meet me on my path of both my marriages which had necessary endings, along with all the growing pains, the moments of bliss, and the dreams and synchronicities all leading to a deeper redemption and freedom. The living inner relationship that I found with my Beloved lit a flame of mystical light that illuminated the way as I followed with one prayer of surrender after another.

> My prince is the Prince of Peace who has a beating, living heart of love for each of us.

The longing to find true love was found not in a person or marriage but in the Divine oneness of Love itself. The terror of losing love, losing attachments, and of being alone only to discover your truth, your true self, and the reality that you are one with all creation, and then return back to ordinary life with new eyes, is nothing short of a miracle. The fire of mystical love takes you into the dark abyss, from yourself and the God you thought you knew, through the exhilaration, the searing desolation, and testing until it has its way with you—until you feel so deeply loved and alive and welcome in that all are truly one. I do have a love story, but not the one I imagined as a little girl watching *Cinderella*. My prince is the Prince of Peace who has a beating, living heart of love for each of us.

May the mystical, the spiritual, and all faith-filled people in every tribe and nation be led to heal the ordinary or extraordinary world they abide in. May we be torch bearers for those in darkness to cheer them through their own personal abyss, where healing and comfort can be available to all. The more present we become to ourselves, the more present we become to others. Ministers can be regular people, like you and me, who love others as themselves.

Henri Nouwen, a well-loved Catholic priest and author, spoke of the wounded healer: "For all ministers are called to recognize the sufferings of their time in their own hearts, and make to that recognition the starting point of their own service. Whether we try to enter into a dislocated world, relate to a convulsive generation, or speak to a dying person our service will not be perceived as authentic unless it comes from a heart wounded by the suffering about which we speak."[2]

On this path you will find allies like I did. They will show up to give you hope and confidence. It may come in the form of a person, like my Jungian professor above who believed in me. Or in a new piece of knowledge and truth you read in a book. Spirit knows what you need and when.

GROWTH AND SERVICE

When my girls were little and I was a stay-at-home mom, I had this little prayer on the fridge about sweeping the floor. All moms with young children know how gross and messy floors can get in a day. It made me, and I'm sure it was grace helping, feel like the smallest thing I did in my day (like sweeping the floor so many times) could be a sacred act.

MY MYSTICAL PATH

It reminds me of Mother Teresa's well-known sentiment about doing small things with love.

I look back now on those days as being so dear and remember how hard it was sometimes. I constantly tell my girls that raising their little ones well is their most important work in life. Having a vocation then to raise a family and to transition to a career that I felt called to is all meaningful service. It is my sincere hope that when you consider all that you do to love and care for another in a day, it may help you feel like an agent of grace and service—be they big or small acts.

Having felt led and called to this unexpected mystical journey, especially in the work I have been privileged to do, has required some patience at times. Once, Don Juan's mother said what felt like an indirect insult that hurt until I recognized her lack of true understanding. She intimated that people who went into my profession did so because they have a lot of problems they are trying to figure out. Maybe there is a bit of truth to this for some; but there are also those who are called to help others psychologically and spiritually, and that is the path that I walk. I am grateful for the healing that came by stepping on that path.

I remember as a girl I would cajole my little sister into being my student. I had a green chalkboard and a teacher's desk set up in our dark basement laundry room where we sometimes played. I've always wanted to be a teacher. I began college majoring in Special and Elementary Education. I was interested in emotionally disturbed children. On the Myers-Briggs personality indicator, I am an INFJ, which is characterized by a gentle, caring, and creative nature. There are sixteen types of personalities that make up the Myers-Briggs. Mine is a rare type—less than 10 percent of the population have this type. INFJs make excellent counselors and teachers, have deep intuition, and can even have a sixth sense about people. We are deep feelers and are introverted.

I had an opportunity, after my mother-in-law's death (Don Juan's mom), to have a reading done. The psychic medium saw my late mother-in-law around me, especially in the mornings when I was praying. The medium said she often had tea with me. I found that interesting and comforting to hear, and I took it all with the proverbial grain of salt. It made me feel that maybe she now respected and was curious about the healing profession I am in.

Giving birth to your true self does require riding the waves of anguish and exhilaration with each contraction until those opposing sides of us unite. Often counsel is needed. Had I not gone through my dark night and embraced my shadow, and instead stayed in my first marriage, I may have allowed a family to stay together. But how does a depressed mom with massive growing pains benefit her children?

Working with many clients, I have seen firsthand how the varying dynamics of growing up with a depressed or ill mother creates codependency and wounds. Those wounds are born out of unmet needs in her child, all because that mother could not be present with her child.

SELF-CARE AND BEING PRESENT FOR YOURSELF

Love never fails. There were times, no doubt, when struggling through my grief and tests, that I had trouble being completely present with my girls, but I did my best to show up for them during painful moments, and I hope they will tell you that I did okay.

I posted a quote by Teresa Shanti recently on my Instagram page. Many liked it and seemed to resonate with it, including one of my daughters. My daughters know and feel how loved they are and how I tried to be there for them. That popular quote read "To my children, I'm sorry for the unhealed parts of me that in turn hurt you. It was never my lack of love for you. Only a lack of love for myself."

MY MYSTICAL PATH

How many of us women can say amen to that? Again, many women can't do what I did; I get that. Today I teach women, and uphold as vitally important, the value of self-care—even and especially if you are a mother. To me it is sacred self-care. My girls know I stand for this, and I see them practicing it in their own lives. My struggle has not been in vain if my life and modeling it brings meaning to them.

The rigors of my graduate program required us to clear the clutter and learn the tools for self-care. For me, or any caregiver who desires to serve and be effective, I believe we must learn this. I had to fight off guilt sometimes when attending classes or workshops. I was used to devoting all my time and energy to the events at home.

This realization happened when a soul sister/colleague and I were driving to a workshop on dreams. My friend and I worked primarily in the field of grief and loss at that time, and understanding the dreams of the bereaved allowed us to serve them better. I loved the learning too. Sarah, my youngest, was staying with her dad part-time then. Calling Sarah and hearing her voice, knowing she was okay, helped quiet the guilt and the voice of her dad in my head calling me selfish while I was attending the workshop with my friend.

Treating myself with gentle respect even in those whirling dark times was a new practice that often felt a bit shaky for me. Standing as the caretaker of my own soul and protecting it was hard when so many didn't understand my path, but there were enough that did. I have come to understand that my or anyone's self-care, self-love, and self-compassion reflects God's love for us.

Teaching myself years ago, and my clients today, how to meditate and how to be mindful is nourishment for the soul. Sitting in that converted classroom meditation room at Loyola in between classes as a new graduate student brought a new, inviting kind of serenity as I and all the colorful, comfy pillows began to get acquainted with the joy of being still.

Creating Your Meaningful Life: Inviting Peace

Prayer, meditation, yoga, a warm detox bath, a pedicure, massage, an acupuncture session, planning a vacation, eating well, juicing, gardening, decorating, writing, reading, working on mosaics, listening to music, burning candles, buying flowers, journaling, taking supplements, etc., are all some of my favorite ways to care for myself. Anything that helps you connect with your deepest self can be sacred self-care. Connection is key, with yourself, with your Higher Power, with your dear ones.

I ask people I work with to tell me what grounds them and brings them back to themselves and gives them energy. These are your sacred self-care practices. Learning to listen to myself and to know what I am thinking and feeling informs me of what I need to give to myself. It could be something as simple as buying myself a new pair of earrings or picking up some takeout on the way home after a long day.

Often, it is a purposeful long meditation time that cares for my inner self. This is what I had to learn, and it is what I love to teach. It may sound simple, but it was painstaking learning as it took time to learn the true value of caring for myself. This care, your practices, slowly become not optional and a way of life after you begin to feel a more grounded and in-control you emerging.

The false self begins dissolving into an alchemy pot of new revelation to uncover the multifaceted true jewel within. Never will I forget those pulses of life and energy running through every cell of my being when I surrendered to my truth for the first time. Taking this deep descent into the unknown and coexisting with the grief stripped me of outward security and attachments; and left me feeling utterly naked and exposed in a way that was healing my shame. How ironic.

I often tell my clients to trust that, even in the tension and anguish of not knowing, or when in deep grief in their own unique cave, there is much happening below the surface. The metaphor of the dormant earth of winter soon giving way to new seedlings and blooms can be encouraging.

MY MYSTICAL PATH

YOUR UNIQUE JOURNEY

The search for love and meaning, that universal hole in the soul that begs to be filled, was my path to find and discover. If we are really honest, isn't it the universal path for each of us? The questions of what, how, where, or with whom make up your own unique true-life story of overcoming. We all have answers to those questions, and that is your story—your hero's journey. What we do with the questions makes all the difference.

Being a mom, a wife, and becoming a healthy therapist while transforming the unexpected; passing tests and experiencing growth that came through my own healing and marital relationships, all were in the process that has created my legacy—whether I like it or not. Can we ever imagine how our legacy will unfold? I think we can work so hard to create the one we need, or have envisioned, but life may bring an alternative plan. Mom used to say, "Life is stranger than fiction," and I think she was right.

Being filled with the Spirit at nineteen and again through the years, and finally learning to love myself, have had incredible meaning because I have made it so. Having cancer at a young age, fierce love for my children, and the love and lessons learned from the Companion, Don Juan, and now my Knight have brought me here to this moment. I never thought I would get married again after the devastation and pain of my second marriage. Yet, it was to be. I met my Knight, Jay, an intelligent and wilderness-loving man who, like me, had been emotionally abused in his marriage.

In spite of that, Jay has worked hard at overcoming his past and has been successful serving, for many years, as an and administrator. We bonded over talking about our pain, life, and our kids and are still recovering together and have become best friends. He is the kindest man I know, and he loves very deeply. I feel safe with him. He is the first man I have loved who is emotionally available. It took me a long time to find a man like that.

Maybe some women who have had emotionally unavailable fathers grow weary of trying to find a partner who can be there for them emotionally. Doing your own work to heal those hurts will help you so much. It's never too late to do the work and be open to love. I hope to grow old with my Knight as we figure out the rest of the story—our journey—together.

A GRACE-FILLED LEGACY

It was a July morning during the COVID-19 pandemic. The sun shone brightly, and the caterers were setting up a brunch under a white tent with a huge hanging pot of pink impatiens hanging from the tent roof. There was a wedding cake and hand-made flower arrangements I had made for the tables. I was ready. I agonized long and hard about getting married again. We had bought a house in the country near where Christen and Amy were raising their families, where my husband had always dreamed of living. It sits on top of a little hill and has huge mature trees, including a weeping cherry tree, hydrangeas, peonies, pink roses, and even window boxes! My gardening paradise. It's an old house with good energy; and it has big windows and gorgeous views.

All of our kids were there minus one daughter and her family who didn't feel safe traveling with the pandemic. We understood. As my daughter Amy said, "When it's time it's time." I couldn't be afraid. I had come so far and, as one friend said, "you are blessed to have found him." I agree. Just our children and a few close relatives attended the ceremony, which my favorite pastor presided over.

Our son-in-law and his brother played the upright bass and a keyboard, filling the country air with jazz music. I wore a short beige and lace dress I had bought a while back for a special occasion. It hung in my closet, unworn, for years. Maybe my guardian angel had given me a nudge that day to buy it.

MY MYSTICAL PATH

I made a little homemade bouquet to carry and put baby's breath in my hair. We walked out of the house and down the hill after posing for a picture by the white fence with the big white tulle bow streamers blowing around the arbor I tied it to. My oldest granddaughter, three at the time, was the only child who came. The other three grandchildren of mine were too little, and Jay's two little granddaughters didn't come due to COVID-19.

Little Ava was extremely intrigued by this wedding, and the fact that her Mimi was getting married. She told her mom that Mimi was marrying her prince. She was the first one I saw entering the tent, and I gave her my flowers. She listened so intently to every word and exchange we had, and she ate the biggest piece of cake. It was a sweet day. No fanfare, just a happy celebration of love and two brave people who found each other and believe in love and second—or even third—chances.

Maybe I took the long way "home," but coming full circle is what has happened. In a grief process that changes us, acceptance of the loss is necessary, but the harder task is to accept your newly changed self. I once told my son-in-law after my second marriage came to an end that I was going to write a book called *Full Circle in Italy*, because Don Juan had both proposed to and discarded me there. I could not conceive of a settled life then. I told my girls I'd get a cat and continue working and become an old cat lady. They laughed because they know me better.

I have embraced all the chapters of my life. God's amazing grace has sustained and kept me floating even when I felt I was drowning. Without that love and life raft He offered, I'm not sure I could have found such meaning in my life. Actually, I am certain I would have sunk.

> In a grief process that changes us, acceptance of the loss is necessary, but the harder task is to accept your newly changed self.

Forgiveness is a process that you cannot force just because some part of you feels like it may be the right thing to do. We do it for ourselves ultimately. I have chosen to forgive my parents' shortcomings, my former husbands, and most of all myself. I pray my children, my grandchildren, and their children will be able to make meaning and experience God's grace as I have.

If my life leaves just a small footprint along that path for them to do just that, I have lived a rich life and . . . even though I have forgiven, I still needed to tell my story so that my experiences could help others as they navigate and recognize the grace that awaits them in their own lives.

FOR EXPLORATION

1. How have you discovered peace on your path and in what ways might you discover more?
2. What call may you be feeling in your soul? What are the feelings that accompany it?
3. Challenge yourself to write about the legacy your life will leave behind you one day.

EPILOGUE

Making meaning of your life and your significant relationships at different seasons of your journey will help you learn from the past to be better informed for the future. This is the best we can do, isn't it? Don't those of us who are parents want to do a little more or better for our children than we experienced ourselves?

We are always growing and evolving until the day we die. What a blessing to be able to use that growth to make someone's life better, and ours too.

You may find, like I have, that there are different times and levels of companionship, seduction, and grace to experience in every relationship. Our own uniqueness will define how much of each of these we need at different stages of our life.

I am grateful for the lessons I have learned at each stage of my healing journey. I have come to discover that we are here to learn to experience and share unconditional love toward God, others, and ourselves. I am still learning these lessons, but I can honestly say that I now have more wisdom for tomorrow's challenges.

The lessons are often challenging. However, go easy on yourself. If your heart is in the right place and you know how to surrender, you will receive the grace you need in God's perfect timing.

When I read *Living a Gentle and Passionate Life* by Dr. Robert J. Wicks, I was deeply moved. At the time he was the chair of the mind, body, and spirit holistic graduate Pastoral Counseling program at Loyola University. I applied to the program soon after reading his book. It had touched my heart and soul so deeply; I knew this was the right next step for me.

I leave you with his words, which are my prayer for you:

"Feeling both joy and pain fully is essential if we are to be truly alive. When we experience pain, doubt and fear, we must not run from it. We must feel it and then let it flow away from us when it is possible. This 'then,' this moment of release, this opening for new possibilities cannot be rushed. It may take years to come but pray God, it doesn't take one second longer than is needed."[1]

Amen.

ACKNOWLEDGMENTS

I give my utmost gratitude to all my teachers, professors, mentors, and healers for coming into my life with their wisdom, in God's perfect timing, to teach me the lessons I needed to learn. And a big thank-you to all my clients who teach me the real meaning of courage.

I especially want to thank Barbara Hall for journeying with me these last years after my second marriage ended. Your light, love, and gifts have made such a difference. A true friend is a rare gift, and I am so thankful for my friends who have stood by me with their unconditional love. You know who you are. To my ancestral family, in heaven, who still cheer me on today, I love you all—until we meet again.

To my Companion and Don Juan for the time we shared and the care, happy times, and hard lessons that helped me bloom.

To those literary angels who taught me so much about writing from my soul and encouraged my story: Your expertise and warmth have been invaluable. To Kelly Notaras, Carolyn Crist, and to my developmental editor Diana Ceres. Diana, your professionalism, guidance, and our soul connection have made this last year of pulling it all together a delightful one. I loved working with and learning from you. My substantive editor, Elizabeth Brown, who put the polish on it and has the most gracious way of speaking through her edits, I thank you sincerely. To work with someone of your expertise and experience has been a true

MY MYSTICAL PATH

blessing. Thank you, Greenleaf Book Group, and your amazing team, for choosing my story and getting it into book form!

To my husband, Jay—the Knight—who believes in me and has given me the space and encouragement to put in the hours: Thank you for your friendship, love, and for making life so sweet.

Thank you to my dear sons-in-law, Timm and Andrew, for being such stellar guys and loving my girls so well. To my sweet grands, Ava, Olivia, August, and Ayden: You are each a gift of love and inspiration. The legacy of family I longed for is seen and felt each day in all of you.

My dear daughters, Christen, Amy, and Sarah: You all are the joy of my life, and I am so proud of the women you have become. May this, my legacy of love to you, your children, and their children, help equip you a little better for life's bumpy roads.

And to my Beloved, lover of my soul, Jesus. Without You I have nothing. With You I have everything. Thank you for pursuing me.

APPENDIX

ARCHETYPES

The archetypes are an inner representation of our outer way of being. They can be called the personalities of the soul and can also be complex to understand or nail down, because they are everywhere. We can find them in art, world literature and mythology, dreams, and fantasies as well as in our own psyche.

Archetypes represent universal images and patterns that are part of the collective unconscious. Our archetypes are deeply personal aspects of our nature, and they are universal. It is said that we inherit archetypes through instinctive patterns of behavior passed down through our ancestors.

Psychiatrist Carl Jung (1875–1961) advanced the concept of archetypes and intended them as tools in his work to understand people and their drives better. He argues that there is no limit to the number of archetypes that can exist.

Generally, the influence of archetypes can be seen in our behavior and how our emotions are triggered and provide us with meaning. They help us understand ourselves better by understanding more about what drives us.

Jung identified twelve primary archetypes that symbolize basic human motivations. Most of us have several archetypes operating in our personality; however, one archetype tends to dominate. Understanding your own archetype and the archetypes of those you are in relationship with adds in gaining insight into the behaviors and motivations of yourself and others.

THE TWELVE COMMON ARCHETYPES

As mentioned above, there are many more archetypes, such as the three I chose to use in this book to represent my husbands. If you are interested in more in-depth study of archetypes, I recommend looking into the writings of author and speaker Caroline Myss, PhD.[1]

The ego types

1. The Innocent—The innocent desires to be happy and get to paradise. Fears doing something wrong or bad. Also known as the utopian, traditionalist, naive, mystic, saint, romantic, dreamer.

2. The Orphan—The orphan desires to connect with others and has a goal to belong. Fears standing out or being left out. The orphan is also known as the regular guy or gal, everyman, the person next door, the good neighbor, and the realist.

3. The Hero—The hero wants to prove his or her worth through courageous acts and uses expert mastery to improve the world. Because of their competence and courage, their greatest fear is to be weak and vulnerable. Also known as the warrior, crusader, the winner, team player, and dragon slayer.

4. The Caregiver—The caregiver's motto is "love your neighbor as yourself." This archetype has a core desire to protect and care for others. The caregiver has a weakness for martyrdom and being

exploited; and has a fear of being selfish. Their talent is their compassion and generosity. The caregiver can also be known as a saint, altruist, parent, and helper.

The soul types

1. The Explorer—Wants to experience a better, more authentic, and fulfilling life. They need the freedom to find out who they are by exploring the world. The explorer can wander aimlessly and can also be true to their soul. Also known as the seeker and the individualist.

2. The Rebel—Believes rules are made to be broken, and they like to overturn what is not working. Their strength is being outrageous with radical freedom. They are okay with disrupting, destroying, or shocking others. They can also be an outlaw, revolutionary, wildman, or misfit.

3. The Lover—Desires intimacy and experience in a relationship with the people they love. They can lose their identity by trying too hard to please others. They strive to become more physically and emotionally attractive. They can exude great passion, gratitude, and commitment. Also known as the partner, friend, sensualist, and spouse.

4. The Creator—Believes it can be done if you imagine it and desires to realize a vision. They use their artistic skill and control to get it done. They can be perfectionists. They are very creative with a fine imagination. Also known as the artist, inventor, musician, or writer.

The self types

1. The Jester—Wants to live in the moment and loves to have a great time. Hates being bored, so using play and jokes and being funny is a good strategy. Trying to find this joy, which they are good at, can waste time. Also known as the fool, trickster, joker, or comedian.

2. The Sage—Desires truth and longs to find it by using intelligence and analysis to understand. Fears being duped or ignorant. Vulnerable to studying details and never acting but has a talent of being wise. Also known as the expert, planner, professional, teacher, and contemplative.

3. The Magician—Likes to make things happen and desires to understand the fundamental laws of the universe. Wants to make dreams come true but can be manipulative. Good at finding win-win situations. Also known as the visionary, inventor, shaman, healer, and medicine man.

4. The Ruler—Wants power and control and uses it to create success. Fears chaos and being overthrown. Can be rigid and unable to delegate. The ruler takes responsibility and is a good leader. Also known as the boss, king or queen, politician, or administrator.

NOTES

INTRODUCTION

1. See Joseph Campbell, *The Hero with a Thousand Faces: The Collected Works of Joseph Campbell* (New York: New World Library, third edition, 2008).
2. Maureen Murdock, *The Heroine's Journey* (Boston and Shaftesbury: Shambala, 1990), quoted in Joyce Rupp, *Dear Heart Come Home* (New York: Crossroad Publishing, 1999), 49.
3. Joseph Campbell, *The Power of Myth*, collaborator Bill Moyers (New York: Anchor Books, 1991), 151.
4. Caroline Myss, *Sacred Contracts* (New York: Three Rivers Press, 2003), 110.

CHAPTER 1

1. James Dobson, *The Strong-Willed Child* (Carol Stream, IL: Tyndale House Publishers, 1985).
2. Eckhart Tolle, *The Power of Now* (Novato, CA: New World Library), 221.

CHAPTER 2

1. All quotations from the Bible will come from the New International Version (NIV).
2. Marianne Williamson, "What is placed on the altar is then altered. Place any burden on the altar to God within your mind & the situation will miraculously change," Twitter, June 12, 2010, https://twitter.com/marwilliamson/status/16046461432.
3. Caroline Myss, *Intimate Conversations with the Divine* (Carlsbad, CA: Hay House, 2020), xv.

4. Samantha Vincenty, "Signs You Might Be a Mystic," *Oprah Daily*, June 17, 2019, https://www.oprahdaily.com/life/a27614027/what-is-a-mystic/.
5. Eben Alexander, *Proof of Heaven* (New York, Simon & Schuster, 2012).

CHAPTER 3

1. Wikipedia: "True Self and False Self," Wikimedia Foundation, last modified January 12, 2023, https://en.wikipedia.org/wiki/True_self_and_false_self.
2. Kahlil Gibran, *The Prophet* (New York: Knopf, 1923), 52.
3. Robert A. Johnson, *Owning Your Own Shadow* (New York: HarperCollins, 1993), 117–118.

CHAPTER 4

1. Kelly McDaniel, *Ready to Heal* (Carefree, AZ: Gentle Path Press, 2012), 85.

CHAPTER 5

1. Lodro Rinzler and Meggan Watterson, *How to Love Yourself (and Sometimes Other People): Spiritual Advice for Modern Relationships* (Carlsbad, CA: Hay House, 2015), 8.

CHAPTER 6

1. U.S. Department of Veterans Affairs, "How Common Is PTSD in Adults?," accessed February 2023, https://ptsd.va.gov/PTSD/understand/common/common_adults.asp.
2. Sandra Brown, *Women Who Love Psychopaths* (Mask Publishing, 2018), 305.
3. See thewisdomoftrauma.com.
4. Thomas Hübl, *Healing Collective Trauma: A Process for Integrating Our Intergenerational and Cultural Wounds* (Boulder, CO: Sounds True, 2020), 27.

CHAPTER 7

1. Brown, *Women Who Love Psychopaths*, 188.

2. Brown, *Women Who Love Psychopaths*, 65.
3. Saint Teresa of Avila, "Prayer of Saint Teresa of Avila," EWTN Global Catholic Network, https://www.ewtn.com/catholicism/devotions/prayer-of-saint-teresa-of-avila-364.

CHAPTER 8

1. Dan Bates, "The 4 Tasks of Grieving," *Psychology Today*, November 8, 2019, https://www.psychologytoday.com/us/blog/mental-health-nerd/201911/the-4-tasks-grieving.
2. Robert J. Wicks, *Touching the Holy* (Notre Dame, IN: Ave Maria Press, 1992), 26.
3. Elisabeth Kübler-Ross, *Death Is of Vital Importance: On Life, Death, and Life after Death* (Barrytown, NY: Station Hill Press, 1995), 35.
4. Pema Chodron, *When Things Fall Apart* (Boulder, CO: Shambhala, 2000), 4.

CHAPTER 9

1. Ron Roth, *The Healing Path of Prayer* (New York: Three Rivers Press, 1997), 109.
2. Evelyn Underhill, *Mysticism* (Seattle, WA: Pacific Publishing Studio, 2011), 5.
3. Caroline Myss, *Entering the Castle* (New York: Free Press, 2007), 343.
4. C.G. Jung, *Modern Man in Search of a Soul* (Eastford, CT: Martino Fine Books, 2017), 57.

CHAPTER 10

1. Anodea Judith, *Eastern Body Western Mind* (Berkeley, CA: Ten Speed Press, 1996), 5.

CHAPTER 11

1. Joyce Rupp, *Dear Heart, Come Home* (New York: Crossroad Publishing Co., 1996), 113.
2. Henri J. M. Nouwen, *The Wounded Healer* (New York: Crown Publishing, 1979), 4.

EPILOGUE

1. Robert J. Wicks, *Living a Gentle, Passionate Life* (Mahwah, NJ: Paulist Press, 1998), 67.

APPENDIX

1. For more on archetypes, see www.treeoflifecounseling.life.

ABOUT THE AUTHOR

DONNA SHIN-WARD, MS, LCPC, is a licensed Clinical Pastoral Psychotherapist and certified Holistic Wellness Coach specializing in grief, trauma, and helping those who have experienced narcissistic, sociopathic, and psychopathic emotional abuse transcend and transform their experience. In her first book, her own inspirational memoir, readers will be infused with their own energy of possibility to stand up to their own internal accusers and real-life abusers.

Through creative narrative and reflection, as mirrored in the universal experience of many people today, she implores readers to rise and embrace vibrant health and wholeness by speaking their hard truth to themselves first and surrendering to the awakenings that come.

Donna believes people are searching for answers on how to really heal, hold, and live with life's unexpected traumas and hurts. Everyone has a story, and we can learn from one another's shared experiences. She understands that despite our varying storylines, we share collective narratives around love, loss, grief, trauma, and spirituality. She tells us that in order to reach the enlightened present moment we must first go into the darkness of grief and create a friendship with both.

Donna is certified in the internationally used and rapidly growing brain/body physiological trauma therapy known as Brainspotting, which brings psychological benefits. Her professional therapeutic work informs her that the deeper trauma must be addressed to heal the pain of collective and generational trauma.

Donna is passionate about the work she does and often shares her deep faith and spiritual lessons as a modern-day mystic to enhance the healing and wholeness of those she serves. She has a thriving private practice in Towson, Maryland, and a growing social media platform. Her own heart-wrenching and heart-expanding experiences ignited her to create her Soul of Healing groups, a program meeting the needs of women in various stages of recovery from emotional abuse.

Donna lives with her husband, Jay, and their puppy, Sophie, who loves to spend time with her four young grandchildren when they visit. Donna will tell you that her biggest accomplishment in life has been to raise her three wise daughters to be so close and connected to each other. They are truly her favorite people.

If this book moved you, I'd be deeply grateful if you shared an honest review on Amazon. Reviews help the story find the right readers who can resonate, find some healing, and be inspired in their own lives.

Thank you for being here,
Donna

www.ingramcontent.com/pod-product-compliance
Lightning Source LLC
LaVergne TN
LVHW091543060526
838200LV00036B/681